LEOPARD VALLEY

LEOPARD VALLEY

A play in three acts

by

A. K. Chesterton

CANDOUR

The A.K. Chesterton Trust

2013

Printed & Published in 2013. First Edition.

ISBN: 978-0-9564669-9-0 (Paperback)
ISBN: 978-0-9575403-0-9 (Hardback)

Website: www.candour.org.uk

A.K. Chesterton in 1957

Foreword

As far as can now be established, Leopard Valley was the second of three plays written by A.K. Chesterton. It was presumably written after his discharge from the army on medical grounds in 1943, and was performed in Southport in 1944. A newspaper review is included within in the appendices.

Two copies of the script have languished in the archives of the A.K. Chesterton Trust for decades. One (and sadly incomplete) appears to be the original 1943 version, while the second is a 1954[1] adaption. Comet aircraft have replaced liners and the Mau Mau are now the native rebels. This version is longer, and to my mind, much better than the original.

Finally, seventy years after it was written, modern technology has enabled us to publish the 1954 adaption of the play. It is presented as originally typed with some missing and abbreviated stage directions. We have, however, taken the opportunity to correct some minor spelling mistakes.

It is exciting for us to be able to publish the first edition of an A.K Chesterton work, and we hope you enjoy reading it.

Colin Todd

The A.K. Chesterton Trust
January 2013

---

[1] This was "produced in Croydon with a less distinguished cast in 1954" according to notes by A.K.'s wife, Doris Chesterton, held in the University of Bath's Chesterton collection (File A19)

Contents

The Characters in order of appearance

CHARLES ROMLEY..A Settler

JIMMY DE LISLE..A Young Settler

CABBAGE.. An African Manservant

VERA FELTON..A Woman Settler

LORD GEORGE TRENTERLEY..........................Remittance Man

DAPHNE SPELTER..A Settler's Wife

DEREK ROMLEY..A Settler

VIVIEN ROMLEY..His Wife

SONGETI...A Native Chief

SYBIL SELWYN...A Visiting Actress

TWO NATIVES..

ACT ONE

Scene One

Living room of DEREK ROMLEY'S bungalow in the Leopard Valley settlement. Although quite well furnished, the place is obviously a bachelor's establishment. At the back are two very wide windows, looking out upon the stoep. Two doors, L & R and one at the back on extreme L as shown in sketch. Entrants by the last named are first seen through the windows as they pass along stoep. TIME – sunset. Enter CHAS ROMLEY – R (veranda) Hangs hat up, followed by CABBAGE with suit-case.

CHAS   Shove it in my room, Cabbage.

CAB   Yes, Baas (Exit CAB L. Enter JIMMY from up L – hands topee on stand).

CHAS   Hullo, Jimmy.

JIM   Hullo, Charles. How's Johannesburg?

CHAS   Foul, as usual. Another lost weekend. Don't know why I trouble to go there. (Enter CABBAGE) Cabbage, fetch Baas de Lisle and myself a drink.

CAB   Yes, Baas.

CHAS   Better still, let's have the bottle in here. And don't forget the cold supper for the bridge party tonight. Lay it out in the dining room.

CAB	Yes, Baas. (Exit CABBAGE, L)
CHAS	(Sits). As I was saying, I don't know why I bother to go to Joh'burg. I'm afraid I don't really love my fellow men – not in the mass, anyway.
JIM	You seem to take a Hell of a lot of pleasing you know. Before you went off for your weekend you were cursing life here in Leopard Valley – bloody backwater that gave you the jitters, and all the rest of it. (Sits)
CHAS	Yes, that is my trouble, rather. Sort of St. Vitus dance. But you don't know how you're going to take to irrigation farming yet. After all, you've only been in Africa a fortnight.
JIM:	I like it all right so far.
CHAS:	(Sprawls in chair – bored) That's nothing to go by. I was happy enough for the first three or four months. However, it may come out all right in the wash. I'll probably settle down in time, and build a house and get married, like Derek. Great Scott! Today's the twelfth. He'll be back from England in precisely ten days with his bride. Poor kid!
JIM:	I thought he was a good deal older than you.
CHAS:	So he is. Oh, no – I was not referring to him. I was pitying his wife.
JIM:	Do you know her?
CHAS:	No, but I know my brother.
JIM:	You're not very complimentary to him.
CHAS:	Wait 'til you meet him, Jimmy my boy. I don't know thought you may get on very well with each other. You'll probably think him the salt of the earth, as indeed he is.
JIM:	What's your trouble, then?

CHAS: I like my salt a pinch at a time. Oh, Derek's alright.
(Enter CABBAGE with tray of drinks and telegram. Puts drinks down and gives CHAS telegram. Exit CABBAGE L).

JIM: I forgot to tell you, that wire came on Saturday.

CHAS: (Opens telegram – reads it, and jumps up)
Merciful Heavens! They'll be back tonight.

JIM: Your brother?

CHAS: (Nodding) Travelling by air, if you please! (Pushes telegram in pocket and paces about). Typical! In such a hurry to get back to the farm that he shortens his honeymoon by a fortnight. Derek all over. I'll bet he's already given the girl a complete list of her duties out here.

JIM: Something of a taskmaster?

CHAS: Oh, he distributes duties as though they were privileges.

JIM: That's one way of looking at them.

CHAS: Here, not you as well, Jimmy. I can't stand two of you in the vicinity. Two agricultural hot-gospellers would drive me to D.T's. (Goes to drink table and pours out 2 W&S). Well, this sudden news is certainly an occasion for a stimulant. (JIMMY rises and takes drink) Cheerio!

JIM: Cheers! (Both drink. JIMMY crosses to) I suppose I had better pack my kit and move down to the Drift Hotel.

CHAS: Not on your life. Derek won't hear of it. He'll love to put you up and train you in the way you should go. Patriarchal complex, you know. (Drops down to   JIMMY sits   ). Damned inconvenient, his returning today. He'll be furious at the things I've left undone that I ought to have done. Not being here to lead the water on Saturday, for instance, in irrigation farming that's a capital offence. And what is more, he'll thoroughly disapprove of my little bridge party tonight.

15

JIM: Who's coming?

CHAS: Trenterley is the chief snag. Lord Trenterley – He's the son of the Duke of Kingsweal. Out here on remittance.

JIM: Farming?

CHAS: Yes, I suppose that would be a courteous description of his activities. (<u>Sits leaning forward</u>). Mostly he farms the hearts of homesick settler's wives. He's now got the quaint idea of turning his place into a limited liability company.

JIM: Is he likely to succeed?

CHAS: Not a dog's change. Another?

JIM: No thanks.

CHAS: (<u>Pouring out drink</u>) Well, needless to say Trenterley is far indeed from being Derek's curly-headed boy.

JIM: Is he narrow-minded about these things?

CHAS: (<u>Comes round and sits settee</u>) No, not exactly narrow-minded. He's got strong views about what we may euphemistically call making one's own doorstep untidy. (<u>Drinks</u>)

JIM: I see. Who else is coming for bridge?

CHAS: Daphne Spelter and the Virgin. Daphne's husband went bust, and has had to clear off the Rand to make some money to keep things going down here. Trenterley was good enough to come forward with his consolations and he's been trotting round with Daphne for some time, though rather less zealously of late. Just as well, if Peter Spelter got to hear about it.......

JIM: Not a complacent husband?

CHAS: Complacent? Peter reminds me of a fellow I used to know in London. A quiet, mild-mannered chap who wore glasses.

16

Nothing out of the ordinary to look at. But, there was something behind his smile – something formidable. I had known him for a couple of years before I discovered that he had won one of the best V.C.'s of the war.

JIM: Is Peter Spelter a V.C.?

CHAS: No. He did pretty well, though. And he has that same formidable quality. I shouldn't like to be in Trenterley's shoes if he got to hear about Daphne.

JIM: What's she like?

CHAS: She's quite pretty and fluffy and cuddly, I imagine. And not altogether without brains. But spiritually a bit slipshod. (Chuckles at himself). Rather like me, in fact.

JIM: Are you fluffy and cuddly?

CHAS: I don't mean that, you ass.

JIM: And the Virgin, who is she?

CHAS: (Rises and puts glass down and leans on table, arms folded) Vera Felton. She's one of the most remarkable characters I've ever met. A woman settler, farming on her own. Takes some doing, that. Never been seen in anything but riding breeches. Derek adores her There's a sort of tacit 'Let's all be public schoolboys together' atmosphere between them. The Virgin is really a damned good sort, and quite astonishingly innocent. You will not be able to credit some of the things she says at times. When the Facts of Life enter the conversation they leave it again as demurely as a troupe of young curates.

JIM: (Laughs) What do you mean, exactly?

CHAS: I can't explain. You'll have to judge for yourself. It is as though she has some filter in her mind, which resolutely rejects the more vivid realities. They just don't impinge. But you'll see. (VERA FELTON appears on Veranda from R. Both rise) Oh, here she is. (<u>Vera is 28, tall and somewhat masculine in</u> <u>appearance, but this is due in a large part to her riding breeches</u> <u>and manner. There is much charm in her breeziness</u>).

VERA: Hullo.

CHAS: Hullo, Vera. This is de Lisle.

VERA: How do you do, de Lisle.

JIM: How to you do, Miss Felton.

VERA: Plain Felton will do. No ceremony with me, if you don't mind.
          (<u>Slaps her legs occasionally and throughout with riding crop</u>).

JIM: Certainly, er – Felton.

CHAS: de Lisle's the new settler, who's bought the land beyond
          Jackson's Drift.

VERA: Well, he looks as though he'll do. Haven't heard anything from
          your major, I suppose?

CHAS: Not half! Derek's coming back tonight by air.

VERA: What! This very night as ever is? Why, that's marvellous. I'm
          dying to see old Romley again. And he's bringing his wife with
          him? (<u>CHAS nods</u>). That'll be interesting. I wonder what she's
          like.

CHAS: Sit down, wont you?

VERA: All in good time. You sit if you want to. (<u>JIMMY sits</u>) I've
          something to get off my chest. I got back from a visit to the
          store earlier than I expected this afternoon, and what do you
          think I discovered? My two house servants and a strange native
          having a brandy drink in my bedroom.

CHAS: WHAT!

18

VERA: 'Strue as I'm standing here, Mister. Johannes was on the settee, and the stranger was sprawling on my bed.

CHAS: On your bed! Of all the bloody cheek!

VERA: Johannes and the man on the bed were wearing blankets.

CHAS: Blankets! God! They must have been 'Beetles'.

VERA: Beetles my foot! Do you think I don't know the difference between a Bantu and a Beetle?

CHAS: Members of the Death Watch Beetle movement, you ass.

VERA: (Slaps her leg, cross to…..) By Jove, I never thought of that. They do wear blankets, don't they? Sort of symbol.

JIM: Who are these people?

CHAS: (Moves to C) A big native secret society, growing enormously, and sowing sedition all over the place. They are getting very strong in the Valley. This is serious, Vera, this business of yours. I had better 'phone the constabulary. (Turns to 'phone. VERA puts foot on settee).

VERA: You haven't heard the whole story. I've told you about Johannes and the man on the bed. But what do you think Habanga was doing? Dancing in the middle of the room – without a stitch on.

CHAS: Whew! By God, if that isn't the giddy limit. Hang on a minute (Goes to 'phone). Hullo, Royal African Constabulary, please.

(VERA paces up and down, waiting) Hullo, is Sergeant Conway there? Oh, that you Conway? Romley here. Can you send somebody along to see us at once? Miss Felton has a report to make… She's had a visit from the Death Watch Beetles… What, many similar reports… Yes, it looks like it… You'll come yourself? Good. (Replaces 'phone and comes down centre) Conway says it looks as if some bad trouble is brewing. There have been other visitations, it seems. He's coming at once.

JIM: Any link with Mau Mau, do you suppose?

CHAS: We are a bit far south for that. But you never know. (<u>DAPHNE and TRENTERLEY enter</u>) Ah, here are Trenterley and Daphne.

(<u>CHAS introduces JIMMY and ad lib greetings. DAPHNE sits on settee. VERA walks up and down L</u>).

TRENT: Well, Charles, what's all the news?

CHAS: Two items of which the least important is that Derek and his wife return tonight.

TRENT: Tonight? (<u>Sits…</u>)

CHAS: Yes, I've had a wire from Kenya. They're coming by air.

DAPHNE: There could scarcely be more important news than that, Charles.

CHAS: I don't know so much. What would you do, Daph, if you went home and found three natives drinking brandy in your bedroom, and one of them prancing around stark naked?

DAPHNE: I should swoon into the completest oblivion, my dear. Why do you ask so silly a question?

CHAS: (<u>Sits</u>) Silly? Tell them, Felton.

VERA: (<u>Who has been walking about L</u>) Not in the least silly, because it's exactly what I found – one stranger on my bed and one servant on the settee, while the other was dancing in his bare skin.

DAPHNE: My dear!

TRENT: Extraordinary. Were they mad? Or drunk?

20

VERA: Certainly not drunk.

TRENT: What did you do?

VERA: I got rid of them with my riding crop.

DAPHNE: What did you say to them? The naked one particularly?

VERA: I told him I had never seen anything like it in my life. (TRENT and CHAS look at each other). I said "How dare you, Habanga, taking off your clothes in my bedroom without my permission, indeed!" (TRENT and CHAS look at each other. CHAS moves up to cover laugh. JIMMY looks puzzled). Then when I'd made him put on his blanket, I drove them all out with a cut apiece.

CHAS: Better look out, Vera. That's why we get pilloried in the English Press. British settlers oppressing the poor African and the rest of it (They laugh).

TRENT: Did they go with a good grace?

VERA: All that happened was that the strange native – he's rather a dignified customer – turned to me after I lashed him and said in the most exquisite English: "There will come a day, Madam, when Africa will no longer have white women running amok with riding-whips!"

CHAS: (Comes down) Impudent hound.

TRENT: Sounds like Songeti.

DAPHNE: What, the man they call the Beetle Chief? How thrilling.

CHAS: I don't know about thrilling. This beetle business is getting a bit thick.

TRENT: Have you let the police know?

CHAS: Yes, Conway's coming down. It should mean six months hard for two of them and a couple of years for the naked gentleman.

VERA: Why should he get more than the others?

CHAS: Well, if you don't know, I certainly can't tell you. Shall we get on with our bridge? (Switches on lights, brings chair from W.T. JIMMY places other chairs and DAPHNE comes to table).

DAPHNE: Let's.

CHAS: We'll probably have time for a couple of rubbers before Derek arrives.

VERA: With Daphne here? Bit of an optimist aren't you?

DAPHNE: I'm afraid I don't quite get that.

VERA: Well, bridge does rather stimulate your vocal cords, don't you think? (They go to the card table). Do you play, de Lisle?

JIM: Only in emergencies. Not very keen I'm afraid. I'll take a stroll around a little later.

(All sit. After shuffling etc. CHAS calls)

CHAS: In that case do you mind having a look at the temperature in the incubators? If the eggs are done in it won't make for the happiest of reunions with Derek.

JIM: Right, I'll see to them.

DAPHNE: Your call, Charles.

CHAS: A spade.

DAPHNE: Talking about spades, reminds me that Peter wants me to have our fowl-pits dug. (To VERA) Have you had yours done yet?

VERA: Months ago. Your call, Trenterley.

22

DAPHNE: Peter keeps writing to tell me to get this done or that done; his whole mind seems to be on the farm. Poor boy, it's a shame he should have to be working in those filthy mines. His heart is here, in Leopard Valley.

TRENT: Did you call a space, Charles?

CHAS: I think so, but it is so long ago I can't be sure.

DAPHNE: When I say his heart is here, I mean with his orange trees and lucerne and prize cockerels and things. I don't seem to matter nearly so much. It's farm, farm, farm, all the time.

VERA: Lucky for him, perhaps. I imagine there wouldn't be much farm left if somebody wasn't thinking about it.

DAPHNE: I do my best. When we had the water on Saturday, I spent the whole afternoon at home, while the land was being irrigated.

TRENT: I pass.

VERA: It's not my business, but how can you do your best when you spend all your time gadding about Trenterley? They tell me you even spend the night with the man.

TRENT: I say! I can't...

DAPHNE: (Pushes her chair back) Really!

CHAS: It's all right, Daphne, you idiot. Don't you know Vera Felton by this time? She hasn't the faintest idea of any implications in that remark.

VERA: I don't see why you should make this fuss, Daphne Spelter. There's no reason why you shouldn't spend the night with him if you want to. Are either of you frightened of sleeping alone?

CHAS: Come, Daphne, pull your chair up and let's get on with the game.

DAPHNE: (Pulls chair to table) You'll agree Charles, that Vera is just a little – shall we say disconcerting?

CHAS: Vera's entirely guileless, aren't you, Vera? The call is one spade, and it's up to you Vera.

VERA: Two diamonds. Besides, I was not getting only at you. Why weren't you here to lead water on Saturday, Charles?

CHAS: For God's sake cut that out, Felton. I'll hear enough about it from Derek. The call is two diamonds.

DAPHNE: Speaking of diamonds reminds me that Peter wants to have a shot at the diggings some time. I should love to dig for diamonds, but Peter says he won't take me because it's a secretive job and I don't know when to hold my tongue. Isn't that a slander?

CHAS: Of course, Daphne darling. But just to repudiate it, don't you think you might stop chattering for a moment, and bid.

DAPHNE: So sorry, darling. Wait a moment. What did you call, George? A spade, wasn't it?

TRENT: I passed.

DAPHNE: I really must concentrate more. Let me see, now, you called a heart, George, so I'll go two hearts.

TRENT: I did nothing of the kind.

DAPHNE: Thrilling suit, hearts! Wont it be fun, meeting Derek's wife? What do you imagine she'll be like, Charles?

CHAS: No idea. It's my call.

DAPHNE: But you must have some idea – some picture in your mind. What sort of a girl would Derek be likely to choose?

CHAS: I cannot imagine Derek choosing any girl. Up to you, Trenterley. I pass.

DAPHNE: Oh, Charles. What a weird thing to say!

TRENT: Three clubs.

DAPHNE: I'm dying to know if she plays bridge, aren't you Vera?

VERA: Haven't thought about it.

DAPHNE: You don't mean to say you're not interested?

VERA: Of course I'm interested, but not about whether she plays bridge. Don't care a damn if she does or doesn't. Is she going to make Derek a good wife – that's more to the point.

JIM: I'll take my stroll now, I think.

CHAS: Don't forget the incubators. And you might see if you can find a game of bridge knocking around outside. Ours has got lost.

JIM: So it seems. (Laughs and exits centre to right)

CHAS: The call is three clubs.

VERA: I pass.

TRENT: Talking about clubs…

CHAS: (Groaning) The disease is catching. Your call Daphne.

DAPHNE: Sorry, I pass.

TRENT: Talking about clubs, have you heard about the fuss over our getting a drink licence for the Tennis Club? The Drift Hotel people are kicking up no end of a row, most unreasonably, I think.

VERA: Why? Providing drinks is their livelihood, while a tennis club's job ought to be to provide tennis.

TRENT: All the same…

CHAS: We <u>are</u> having an absorbing game, aren't we? (<u>Car noise.</u> <u>Throws cards down</u>) Hullo! The hour has struck.
(<u>CHAS runs out followed by Vera C to L</u>)

DAPHNE: Derek!

CHAS: None other. (<u>Goes running out, followed by VERA centre to L</u>)

TRENT: (<u>Crosses to… Daphne to…</u>)
Well, here they are, Daphne. I don't imagine Romley will be overjoyed to see us. We had better take the first excuse that offers to make a graceful retirement.

DAPHNE: I don't know, George. Perhaps now he's married he won't be so straight-laced. He's a dear, really.

(<u>Voices off. Enter Derek and Vivien. Vera remains on step</u>)

DEREK: Come in dear. Good evening Mrs Spelter.

DAPHNE: Hullo, Derek. We're all so thrilled to see you back. And this is your charming wife?

(<u>Daphne approaches and shakes hands</u>)

DEREK: Yes, this is Vivien. Mrs Spelter, Vivien.

VIV: How do you do.

DEREK: Good evening, Trenterley. Still here, tilling the soil, eh?

TRENT: A charming compliment from you, my dear Romley.

DEREK: This is Lord Trenterley, Vivien.

26

VIV: How do you do. (<u>TRENT approaches and shakes hands</u>).

DEREK: I'll go and see to things (<u>Exits</u>)

TRENT: I'm afraid you didn't expect to find your new home crowded out, Mrs Romley. We'll beat our retreat.

VIV: Oh, please don't. It's great fun meeting people so soon. Won't you all sit down?

            (<u>Enter CHAS. TRENT moves away eyeing Vivien</u>)

DAPHNE: We mustn't stay long.

CHAS: Vivien will want you to stay to supper, I'm sure. It's all ready.

VIV: Oh, good, I'm famished.

CHAS: I arranged a supper because Cabbage is not very good on dinner parties. Cabbage is your cook Vivien.

VIV: Yes, Derek has told me about him. What a heavenly name.

CHAS: But not a heavenly cook. Supper's laid out in the dining room. It's a smash and grab affair. If you'd like to lead the way, Vivien. It's through there (<u>Points R</u>)

            (<u>Exit Vivien, Daphne, Vera and Trenterley. Chas is just about to follow as Derek enters</u>)

DEREK: Well, Charles old fellow, how are things?

CHAS: Ambling along pretty well, I think, Derek. The orange trees are still growing, you know, and you still have about a thousand head of poultry. I don't think my stewardship has been too disgraceful.

DEREK: I'm sure it hasn't. (<u>Gets a drink and mixes one for Charles</u>) Having one?

CHAS: You bet. Would I be so unkind to this auspicious hour as to say no? That's about it, thanks. The Beetles are playing up a bit, by the way. (Takes his drink).

DEREK: I guessed they would do that, sooner or later. This fellow, Songeti, has to be watched. He's going to loom large in Leopard Valley. And far beyond. (PHONE rings. Derek answers. CHAS sits). Hullo! Yes, Romley speaking... No, Derek Romley... Yes, I'm back... Who's that... Oh, yes, Doyle... What's that... Conway has? Good God!... Where?... On the way here....Why?.... My brother? Yes, I'll ask him... Yes very well. Yes, come over in the morning. (Puts down receiver and crosses to centre). Conway has been found dead a hundred yards from the Drift.

CHAS: (Sits up) God!

DEREK: Killed by a spear.

CHAS: Songeti's men – the Beetles.

DEREK: Yes, almost certainly. Doyle says he was on the way to see you in answer to a 'phone message.

CHAS: Yes, I phoned on behalf of Vera. Three natives in blankets – Beetles obviously – staged a brandy drink at her place. She found them in her bedroom, one stark naked. So I asked Conway to come down. I'm sure one of them was Songeti himself.

DEREK: That ought to get him a stretch even if they can't pin poor old Conway's murder on him. Wily bird, not like him to play into the hands of the law.

(Derek puts glass down as JIMMY rushes in from R).

JIM: I say, Charles, the incubator lamps are all out (sees Derek) Oh, I'm sorry.

28

CHAS: (Rises, moves up. Rather embarrassed) This is Jimmy de Lisle, Derek.

DEREK: How do you do. (They shake hands) A new settler?

JIM: Yes.

CHAS: He's bought the land beyond Jackson's Drift, and I've asked him to stay here until his house is built.

DEREK: Splendid! Have a drink, de Lisle. This is great news. (Pouring out drink) We want settlers of the right stamp. Say when…

JIM: Thank you.

DEREK: What's this about the incubator lamps?

CHAS: I'm sorry, Derek. It's probably my fault.

DEREK: Well, you'd better see to them. If the eggs have not been cold too long, it may be all right. Apply the light test.

CHAS: I will. (Finishes drink and exits)

DEREK: Sit down, de Lisle. (Jimmy sits) As I was saying, we want settlers of the right sort. Stickers. It's a good life if a man has the right stuff in him. And not without its excitement.

JIM: So I gather. These Beetle people, for instance.

DEREK: You've heard about them?

JIM: A little. I should like to hear more.

DEREK: That wish is easily gratified, I'm afraid. They've just killed Conway.

JIM: Great Scott! The police sergeant?

DEREK: (Nodding) At least everything points to them. Conway's murdered, at all events. (Sits)

JIM: I say! Things are beginning to hum. Who are the Beetles exactly? I asked Charles whether he thought they had anything to do with Mau Mau, but he wasn't quite sure. Said we were a bit far south for that.

DEREK: Difficult to tell. Shouldn't think so. Mau Mau's a Kikuyu affair. African troubles tend to conform very much to pattern. There was the rebellion of the madman Enoch in the Cape some years ago. It had many features in common with the Maji Maji revolt against the Germans in Tanganyika at the beginning of the century, as well as with that rumpas in Kenya shortly before the Mau Mau business began. In each rising, for instance, the poor dupes were fully persuaded by their leaders that the white man's bullets would turn to water. This showdown here has some distinctive features. It was evidently started by a man who knew something about the Death Watch Beetle in old English churches. They call themselves the prophets of the White Man's Downfall. It's becoming an extensive organisation with many branches. A kind of coloured confederation, with the slogan "Africa for the Africans". It will have to be watched for Mau Mau affiliations, of course.

           (Vera enters with cup of tea and sandwich. Sits) Oh, Vera, there's very serious news. Don't say anything to Vivien just yet, I don't want her alarmed. Conway has been murdered.

VERA: Murdered!

DEREK: Yes.

VERA: Poor fellow. (Pause) Romley, the police must arrest Songeti. If Conway's murdered, I'm positive it must have been his work.

DEREK: I think so too, but I expect he's covered his tracks.

VERA: Well, I'm convinced it was he who entered my house today. Have you heard about that?

DEREK: Charles told me. You can identify him if you see him again?

VERA: Of course I can.

DEREK: That's good. We'll get a warrant issued in the morning.

JIM: What I don't understand is the motive for that little episode in
            Miss Felton's house.

DEREK: I've been thinking about that, too. The explanation is something
            like this: Songeti is the titular chief of the Amaloba – or what
            remains of them. They were a great warrior race years ago.
            Now they live in a big location a couple of miles from here,
            half of it in the native reserve. From there he seems to be
            carrying out an irredentist policy, roping in the farm labourers
            and house boys throughout Leopard Valley Settlement, and
            beyond. Most of them are his spies, although not Cabbage. At
            least, I don't think so. No, of course not. Cabbage and I are
            great friends. He was the first hand I engaged, you know. The
            two of us hacked down the bush, shoo'd off the elephants, put
            up the fences, did almost all the pioneering work together. He
            has put as much into the farm as I have. Only when we became
            established, so to speak, did his ambitions soar beyond the
            lucerne and the citrus to reach the dizzy heights of the kitchen.
            Came to me one day and said he wanted to be my cook-boy. I
            sent him for instruction to a hotel in Flensburg. No doubt the
            hotel people did their best, but poor Cabbage was not born to be
            Mrs Beeton's curly-headed boy.

VERA: He's got the curly-head all right.

DEREK: But not the flair.

VERA: That's putting it mildly. Why not face the fact that he's a
            perfectly ghastly cook. People in the Valley are very fond of
            you, Derek Romley, but if there's one thing they dread more
            than a visit from Songeti's men, it's an invitation to dine in this
            house.

DEREK: I suspected as much. However, Cabbage thinks himself the cat's whiskers as a chef and I haven't the heart to disillusion him. My friends will simply have to put up with his lack of culinary genius. (<u>To Jim</u>) Bad luck on you, I'm afraid.

JIM: (<u>Laughing</u>) I can take it.

DEREK: I remember the first cake he made. Put forty eggs into it. (<u>They laugh</u>). Just as well we run a thousand head of poultry. However, to return to more serious things. This fellow Songeti is still very much a mystery man. So far he has been working in the dark. None of the settlers has ever seen him – except Vera perhaps. And that little business probably means that he's trying to rid the natives of their awe of their masters by making them disport themselves in the houses of the white men. Teaching them contempt.

JIM: I see.

VERA: I think you're probably right.

DEREK: By the way, Vera, have you a revolver?

VERA: I have not.

DEREK: Then I'll let you have one.

VERA: Shouldn't know how to use the thing.

DEREK: (<u>Rises and puts glass on table</u>) I'll teach you in the morning. What is more, I'm going to ask de Lisle to go back with you tonight and sleep at your place for a bit.

JIM: I'll do that with pleasure.

VERA: You'll do nothing of the kind.

DEREK: I insist.

VERA: Insist 'til you're blue in the face. Have you thought about my reputation?

DEREK: Er – no. To tell you the truth I'd forgotten that aspect. But even so...

VERA: "Even so" my eye. My reputation means a lot to me.

DEREK: Of course it does. I'm sorry.

VERA: Do you think I am going to have myself pointed out all over the Settlement, with people raising scornful fingers at me, saying "Do you see that woman? That's Vera Felton. She had young de Lisle to sleep with her because she was terrified of sleeping alone"? (Rises and puts cup on table) Oh, no.

DEREK: (Smiling) If that's your objection we needn't worry very much.

VERA: I say no. My will is as strong as yours.

DEREK: Look here, old girl, either you put de Lisle up for the night or we'll have to take it in turns to come over and keep watch outside your house. I mean it.

VERA: Very well, blast your sweet eyes, if you put it like that.

(Enter CHAS, very sheepishly)

CHAS: I'm afraid the eggs are washed out, Derek. Damn sorry, old man.

DEREK: Well, there it is.

CHAS: You can dock it out of my share if you like.

DEREK: Can you compute the value of those chickens and all their posterity? (Rises) We'll call it an Act of God. (CHAS moves up to step – as Derek goes to desk and picks up letter) Hullo, what's this? What's this, Charles? (Reads) "Dear Sir, This is to confirm your telephoned refusal of water supplies on August

33

12th. Signed Piet van Rooyen, Conservancy Officer". (<u>Derek approaches Chas then down to ....staring at letter. VERA puts finger to lips and beckons JIMMY out R</u>).

CHAS: (<u>Comes down</u>) I really am damned sorry, Derek.

DEREK: Had all the rain you want, here?

CHAS: Far from it, I'm afraid.

DEREK: Then what the blazes did you mean by refusing water supplies?

CHAS: Incredible slackness on my part, I admit.

DEREK: Slackness! How do you think an irrigation farmer is to keep alive if he refuses his water supply? (<u>Paces about</u>) God, if you had been with me from the beginning and knew what it is to encounter drought, you wouldn't be such an unconscionable B.F. Drought, Charles. Ever heard of it? It means no crops. Do you consider that a trifle? It means dead cattle, dead poultry, withered orange trees. At the best it means the wiping out of years of work, the necessity of starting the whole God-forsaken business of development all over again. At the worst it means calamity, ruin, having to clear out and get a job on the mines. Why can't you be your age? (<u>Abruptly</u>) Johannesburg, I suppose.

CHAS: Yes.

DEREK: H'm (<u>Goes to 'phone</u>) Is there any water still coming down?

CHAS: I don't know. Unlikely, I should say.

DEREK: (<u>Phoning</u>) Give me the Conservancy Officer. What's that, disconnected – Oh! Right, thank you. (<u>Puts down receiver</u>) Line cut!

CHAS: The Death Watch Beetles.

34

DEREK: Not unlikely. (To Chas) Look, take a horse and get up into the mountains. You'll arrive at old du Plessis' place by one, and he'll give you a shake down for a few hours. Then ride on to the dam and see what you can fix up with van Rooyen.

CHAS: You don't mean tonight?

DEREK: I do mean tonight.

CHAS: Have you gone completely batty? Up those mountain treks!

DEREK: It'll be moonlight, and I've had to do it in the early days without a moon. Get some supper and then get off.

CHAS: Don't you think you might have a heart, Derek?

DEREK: Have a heart? When the entire future of this farm, and of everybody on it, may depend on that water?

CHAS: In that case I suppose you wouldn't contemplate making the trip yourself?

DEREK: You stagger me Charles, absolutely stagger me. You are a partner in this business, you have a responsibility towards it. If you betray that responsibility by clearing off for a weekend in Johannesburg when you should be water-leading, then it's up to you to put things right, if you can. To suggest that I should make up for your own slackness is sheer blistering impudence.

CHAS: You talk about responsibility. Are you prepared to take the responsibility of sending me to my death?

DEREK: Your death. Don't talk like a hysterical schoolgirl.

CHAS: Does it strike you that I will have to go past Songeti's location? Where Conway was done in?

DEREK: Charles, I refuse to get panicky! If I did, I should never leave that front door for fear of a spear in the back. Pull yourself together, man. A settler can't wrap himself in cotton wool.

35

Besides, I think Songeti's crowd will be satisfied with Conway for a day or two. In any case, if the worst comes to the worst you'll have your gun and a chance to shoot it out. Coming in for supper before you go?

CHAS: No, thanks.

DEREK: Please yourself – about supper.

          (Exit DEREK R. CHAS has a drink of neat whisky. Enter TRENTERLEY)

TRENT: Not eating?

CHAS: No. Trenterley, how would you like to go riding into the mountains tonight?

TRENT: Not at all, thank you. I may not have an elegant neck, but I'm attached to it. Why?

CHAS: My unspeakable brother insists on my going. But I'm not going to do anything of the kind. Look here, Trenterley, it will be all right if I start in the morning, do you think you could put me up for the night?

TRENT: With pleasure, my dear fellow. You'll find everything ship-shape and a pair of pyjamas in the chest of drawers. (Fumbles) And here's the key of the side door.

CHAS: Thanks very much, old man. You're a brick. But why the key? Aren't you coming?

TRENT: No. (Looks at door and lowers voice). Pressure of business elsewhere, Charles. Strictly between you and me, of course.

CHAS: (Grinning) Of course.

TRENT: I don't know why in these modern times, Leopard Valley should frown on one's private arrangements, but frown it certainly does. Your brother's influence, I suppose.

CHAS: Look, Trenterley, I've got my own ideas about Derek's standards, but he's not the prig you're trying to make him out to be. He's not in the least a prig, really.

TRENT: Charming loyalty – especially when it follows so closely on the delightful little midnight jaunt he proposed for you.

CHAS: Yes, blast his eyes. And yet – and yet, Trent, Derek's right, dead right.

TRENT: Ah well! Goodnight, old boy, sleep well.
(Chas waves farewell. Exit Chas to .... picking up sun-hat. All enter, talking and laughing. Trent to....)

VERA: Well, we must be off. (Trent gets hat. Derek enters). Got your toothbrush packed, de Lisle?

JIM: Yes, here (In pocket)

DAPHNE: You're not going away, Jimmy, are you?

JIM: No – not exactly.

DAPHNE: Whatever do you mean by "not exactly"?

VERA: He's sleeping with me if you must know.

DAPHNE: Oh, congratulations.

(Derek, Trent, and Jimmy laugh. Derek joins Vivien who is looking out of the window)

JIM: You're the limit, Mrs Spelter.

DAPHNE: But why?

VIV: What a lovely scene – the moonlight in the Valley and the great mountains beyond, and all the trees. Orange trees, I suppose?

DEREK: Among other. Do you think you are going to like it here, my dear?

VIV: Darling! I'm adoring it already. It's perfect. We're going to have a lovely life, Derek. (Hyaena howl) What was that?

DEREK: Only a hyaena.

VIV: How thrilling! Oh, I'm going to be happy, happy, happy.

VERA: We're all off now, Vivien.

DEREK: We'll see you home, Vera. It's a grand night and I'd like Vivien to see the groves from your stoep. We'll be back in an hour, Vivien. Are you game?

VIV: Rather!

DEREK: Not too tired?

VIV: Of course not, darling. I'm much too thrilled and happy to be tired. Shall I put on a hat?

DEREK: Great Scott, no. Come as you are and enjoy the evening breezes. (Comes down steps) Are we all fit?

TRENT: We are. We go part of the way, Mrs Romley.

           (All chatter and exit as CABBAGE enters with tray for glasses)

DEREK: I'll join you in a jiffy. (Comes down) Well, Cabbage, here I am again.

CAB: Yes, Baas.

DEREK: How have things been going?

CAB: They go well, Baas.

DEREK: Good. Wife and picaninnies well?

CAB: (Proudly) I got two wives now, Baas.

DEREK: Two! Why, you reprobate, the Mfundas came and baptised you only a few days before I went to England.

CAB: Yes Baas, I very good Christian.

DEREK: A good Christian is faithful to one wife.

CAB: I better Christian, Baas. I faithful to two wives.

DEREK: (Smiling to himself) Immemorial Africa!

CAB: I no understand Baas.

DEREK: Skip it.

CAB: Skip it, Baas? Like picanninies with a rope?

DEREK: If you like. All right, Cabbage. Lock the place up when you're done and turn in if you want to. I've got a key.

CAB: Yes, Baas.

(Exit Derek. CABBAGE up on stoep and watches them off. Hurries to door L and backs away with a gasp of terror. SONGETI and two natives enter, all three dressed in blankets. SONGETI is tall, handsome, with a beautiful speaking voice. His command of English is absolute).

SONG: Well, indunas, here we are. Make yourselves at home. (Indicates chairs and natives sit on settee) (To CABBAGE) You will serve us with drinks, M'Tosi.

CAB: Yes, Inkoos. (Goes to table and seizes bottle).

SONG: Not that Cape dop, I beg of you. You are to serve me, your chief Songeti, a great and educated man. And a great and educated man drinks only the best Scotch Whisky.

39

CAB: Yes, Inkoos. (<u>Is terrified and gets another bottle from sideboard, returns to table and pours out drink</u>) I fear the Baas Romley's anger Inkoos.

SONG: And has your own chief no anger for you to fear, M'Tosi?

CAB: Yes, Inkoos.

SONG: Then that is well. Now you will serve me first. (<u>Cabbage hands Songeti glass, hand trembling</u>) That is right. Now these great indunas. (<u>Cabbage gives drinks to natives</u>) Good. And now you will drink yourself. You have my permission.

CAB: Yes, Inkoos. (<u>Pours himself a drink</u>).

    (<u>SONGETI raises his glass and drinks. Others drink and CABBAGE sips</u>).

SONG: Now you will go and put your blanket around you and when you come back I will summon up in you the fighting blood of your ancestors, and you will cast off your blanket and dance the war-dance of your warrior sires.

CAB: Yes, Inkoos.

SONG: Because there will come war again in the land, M'Tosi, you understand.

CAB: Yes, Inkoos.

SONG: Good. (<u>Drinks, and then speaks</u>) This is really extraordinarily good whisky.

<u>CURTAIN</u>

ACT TWO

SCENE ONE

**The same. Evening. Six months later. Lights on. Drinks on sideboard.
Flowers on tables and curtains to windows. Cushions etc.**

**VIVIEN lies on settee, reading book.
JIMMY enters – hangs up hat and comes in.**

JIM: Hullo, Vivien, Derek not back?

VIV: No. He's still at the settler's meeting. Probably having a hectic argument. Poor Derek, he does take the Settlement life seriously.

JIM: Good thing he does, Vi. Leopard Valley would never be as prosperous as it is without him. (<u>Sits</u>)

VIV: (<u>Rises and puts book on bookcase and returns and sits on settee</u>) You mean organising and that sort of thing?

JIM: Yes. I'm told that at first every man was selling against every other man, and they all allowed themselves to be rooked by the buyers. Now there's a Leopard Valley Egg Board, and a Leopard Valley Citrous Board and so on. Working together. But I believe Derek found it the devil's own work to get the silly asses to co-operate. Now he's trying to improve the Dairy stock by importing a bull for the Settlement, but it'll take months and months before they see his point. It's being brought up at today's meeting.

VIV: Why aren't you there supporting him?

JIM: Oh, jobs about the place, you know.

VIV: Don't lie, Jimmy. You've had nothing to do since four.

JIM: Well, if you must know, Derek asked me to hang about and look after you.

VIV: Look after me!

JIM: Don't get alarmed, but things are beginning to hum again. Songeti's been out of jail for three weeks.

VIV: Oh, that Death Watch Beetle business.

JIM: I wish they'd been able to fasten poor old Conway's death on the swine. But they'll get him one day, don't worry.

VIV: It all seems very stupid – and a bit horrible. I don't know why anybody should want to live in a country where there are such beastly men. I rather agree with Charles there, I'm afraid.

JIM: Charles back from Joh'burg?

VIV: Not yet. You know, it struck me that Derek was a little unreasonable about his Johannesburg trip. After all, Charles is young and its only natural that he should get bored stiff with the Settlement at times. Don't you think so, Jimmy?

JIM: Yes – I suppose so.

VIV: You said that as though you had some reservations.

JIM: I don't know. It's not for me to say. I like Charles. But I do think he should make up his mind either to put his back into it or else clear out.

VIV: I'm afraid it will come to that – clearing out, I mean. Oh, I'm dreading the clash that's sure to come – the final bust up. You know, I'm convinced that Derek doesn't come within a hundred miles of understanding Charles.

JIM: Curious you should say that, because I'm equally certain that Derek understands him perfectly.

VIV: Well – don't think I'm criticising my husband, I adore him as you know – but if what you say is true, why is he so – so, what shall I say? – so stern with him?

JIM: Because he realises that Charles, like everybody else, has got to come to some kind of terms with life. He had to do it himself. So have we – you and I. We may be lucky in being able to do it more easily, but we're both adjusting ourselves quite satisfactorily.

VIV: I wish to Heaven I were.

JIM: What!

VIV: No, it was stupid of me to have said that. Forget it Jimmy, there's a dear. I'm getting on quite well really. After all, life's not so bad. There's tennis twice a week. And bridge. And an occasional gymkhana. Besides, Derek's been sweet about giving me breaks at the seaside. And once at the Victoria Falls. I ought not to complain.

JIM: You don't find the farm interesting?

VIV: Oh, yes, the chicks are sweet when they're a day or two out of the incubators and its fun seeing so many of them about at the same time. And I like the horses. Various things like that I find interesting.

JIM: But not the actual farm-work? Why not take over the Incubator Department?

VIV: Don't go putting ideas like that into Derek's head (Pause). No, Jimmy, I can't say I find hard work of any kind interesting. Does anybody, in his secret heart?

JIM: You're pulling my leg

VIV: No, I'm not, truly. People like Derek are an exception. Most of us surely find work tedious and abominable, to be avoided wherever possible. And to do a real job of work in a climate like this... I ask you! It isn't a very jolly place, is it Jimmy? Be honest!

JIM: I think it is very jolly.

VIV: Even with the Beetles lurking everywhere?

JIM: We'll put the Beetles where they belong before we've done with them.

VIV: I only hope you're right. They make life unbearable. As you know, my one real passion is riding, but Derek won't let me go more than a ten minute trot from the house. I'm sure it's not as dangerous as all that, at any rate in the day time.

JIM: Derek's right not to let you take risks. Even if there were no Beetles, one has to ease oneself gently into Africa. It's a queer place, full of situations we're not trained to meet. But Africa grows on one.

VIV: "Grows on one" – merciful Heavens.

JIM: It does on me, at all events. Don't you feel fascinated at the job that has been done here, for instance? A few years ago Leopard Valley was a semi-desert. When the infrequent rains came they roared down the water-courses and were gone in a jiffy. Now the great dam has been built high up in the mountains and we have the water whenever we want it for our crops. That's an achievement, surely. Look at the result! Look out there! Isn't it a gorgeous sight?

VIV: Your ardour is sweet, Jimmy. But I can't pretend that these things thrill me in the very least. (Pause). (ENTER CHARLES. Hangs up hat and crosses to.....) Well, Charles, we know the form, I am going to ask you how's Joh'burg, and you're going to reply "Foul, as usual".

44

CHAS: Quite right, foul, as usual (<u>Jimmy and Viv laugh as Charles gets a drink from sideboard</u>) The dullest continent God ever conceived. (<u>Crosses to chair and sits as CABBAGE enters with bag and exits L. Returns and exists L veranda. Vivien gives a little shudder as Cabbage enters and watches him in and out.</u>)

CHAS: Hullo, Jimmy.

JIM: Hello.

VIV: Poor old Charles, don't you find any virtues in all Africa?

CHAS: Oh yes. It provides air fields from which Comets take off for Europe. (<u>All laugh</u>) Trenterley been in?

JIM: No, but he said he was dropping in for a sundowner when I saw him.

CHAS: Yes, I arranged it before I left. I've been showing that prospectus of his to more Joh'burg sharks and he's coming to learn the news.

VIV: Is there any?

CHAS: Yes, the ugliest chorus of laughter you ever heard.

VIV: I wonder why he's so keen for the company to be formed.

CHAS: To get it to hold the baby, while he foots it for pastures new, I suppose. Wise man. God, how my own heart sank when I saw the Valley again. Don't think I'll be able to stick it much longer.

VIV: Oh, Charles.

CHAS: Must face up to it, Viv. I'm not cut out for the job. It's all right for you two. You've got the guts to stay and make a success of it. It's obvious you're both as happy as the day is long.

VIV: (<u>Jumps up</u>) For God's sake, shut up, Charles! Oh, I'm sorry. I didn't mean – (<u>rushes out R weeping. Both jump up – ad lib</u>)

JIM: I say, Vi.

CHAS: What the…. What's biting Vivien?

JIM: Haven't the faintest.

CHAS: God! If it isn't bad enough without people becoming temperamental. (<u>Enter DAPHNE</u>) Hullo, Daphne.

DAPHNE: Hullo. Any sign of George?

CHAS: No, but I'm expecting him any moment. He's coming to hear about the prospectus.

DAPHNE: I suppose that's why he said he'd meet me here. We're dining at the Brown's.

CHAS: I'm glad you arrived first. I wanted a word with you.

JIM: I must go and wash. (<u>Exit R</u>)

DAPHNE: With me? Whatever about? (<u>Sits</u>)

CHAS: (<u>Sitting on edge of table</u>) I ran into Peter in Joh'burg.

DAPHNE: Oh, did you? How is he?

CHAS: I got the idea that he's a bit….

DAPHNE: Well?

CHAS: A bit on guard.

CHAS: You don't suppose anybody has written from the Valley tipping him off, do you?

DAPHNE: Tipping him off? I don't follow.

46

CHAS: Who's fencing now?

DAPHNE: Then come to the point. What did Peter have to say about me?

CHAS: Oh, not a word; apart from asking how you were.

DAPHNE: Then why all the mystery?

CHAS: It was nothing he said about you, or about anybody else, if it comes to that. But he was telling me of a mine manager on the Rand who wants to buy land down here, and so, of course I mentioned Trenterley's prospectus.

DAPHNE: Yes, go on.

CHAS: At the mention of Trenterley I noticed a gleam come into Peter's eye – it was frightening, rather.

DAPHNE: (Laughing) Silly boy! I know he doesn't like George, but all the same Peter's awfully tolerant and understanding. There isn't a gentler person in the world.

CHAS: You're wrong, Daphne. Dead wrong.

DAPHNE: You won't mind my saying so, Charles, but I do know my own husband rather better than you do. (Enter TRENTERLEY, hangs up hat)

TRENT: Hullo, Daphne. We're a bit late. I just went to hear about the prospectus, Charles. We're dining out.

CHAS: Have a drink, at least. (Gets 2 drinks – sherry)

TRENT: That's an idea. (Sits settee) Well, what about that old prospectus?

CHAS: (Gives drinks to Daphne and Trent and returns to chair and sits) I showed it to the people you mentioned.

TRENT: Yes?

CHAS: I'm afraid I was rewarded with a bitter look.

TRENT: I'm sorry. What did they say?

CHAS: Not fit to repeat. But it seems that he people with a passion for investing money in citrus farms are now all financially exhausted.

TRENT: Don't know about that. I must fix it somehow.

CHAS: Why not turn your land over to tomatoes?

DAPHNE: Tomatoes? Are they profitable?

TRENT: Why tomatoes?

CHAS: Well, you see, the tomato is not easy to grow, packs badly, and is difficult to keep. On those grounds alone its propagation ought to appeal to a vast multitude.

TRENT: Getting cynical in your old age?

DAPHNE: Old age! I was thinking that you were much too young to be as clever as you are, Charles. You haven't got the chassis to support it.

CHAS: That's quite the profoundest thing you've ever said, Daphne! However, there it is, Trenterley, I'm sorry.

TRENT: Well, thank you for trying, Charles. (Rises and puts glass on bookcase as DEREK and VERA enter). Here's Derek with the Virgin.

(Derek hangs hat up. DAPHNE rises. CHASE rises and takes her glass)

DEREK: Hullo. Another meeting?

48

DAPHNE: We're just off, Derek.

VERA: Trenterley, why weren't you at the Settler's meeting?

TRENT: Couldn't work up any enthusiasm, I'm afraid.

VERA: You should have been there to support Derek's community bull.

TRENT: What community bull is that?

CHAS: Nothing personal, Trenterley.

(All laugh. Daphne talks to Charles)

DEREK: Well, I'm surprised to hear you all tell Trenterley that, Vera, considering you voted against me yourself. Why did you by the way?

VERA: Well, to tell you the truth, Derek, I think you've got a bee in your bonnet about this bull business.

DEREK: In what way?

CHAS: This ought to be good.

VERA: I can't for the life of me see why we want a bull when there are so many oxen about.

(Chas and Trent turn away to laugh)

DEREK: Look here, Felton, I had better explain to you that oxen are treated in a way which makes them biologically incapable of deputising for a bull.

VERA: Really! That does surprise me. Why didn't you tell me that before?

DEREK: Well, I imagined....

VERA: And why didn't you tell the Settlers that? I'm positive they don't know. Chapman, for instance. I'm certain Chapman doesn't know. I'll phone him up and tell him the moment I get back.

DEREK: Vera, you will do nothing of the kind.

VERA: I certainly will. If we'd only known we'd have been for the bull every time.

DEREK: I don't want you to say anything to Chapman.

VERA: I'm sorry, but he must be made to understand the position. It's only fair to you. I'll go off and do it at once. Goodnight all (Exits slapping her leg)

DEREK: (Racing after her) Vera!

(As soon as she goes, they all laugh. DEREK returns, stop laughing – Derek stands a moment and smiles – then ALL roar with laughter)

DEREK: (Coming down steps) Extraordinary, isn't it?

TRENT: Well – ha, ha, ha – well, we must be off now – ha, ha, ha. Come, Daphne, my dear. (Daphne up on to stoep. Trent gets hat and is about to go as Derek stops him) Ha, ha, ha, what a joke to tell the Browns' tonight.

DEREK: I shouldn't if I were you.

TRENT: They'll roar. (Going out. Derek follows and swings him around)

DEREK: Trenterley, I'd be obliged if you did not repeat what has been said.

TRENT: All right, all right, ha, ha, ha.

DAPHNE: Goodnight, everybody.

ALL: Goodnight. (<u>Exit Daphne and Trent</u>)
(<u>As soon as they go they laugh heartily – and fades</u>)

DEREK: Where's de Lisle?

CHAS: Having a bath, I think.

DEREK: (<u>Sits….</u>) What's the news in Johannesburg?

CHAS: (<u>Sits…. With a growl</u>) Leopard Valley.

DEREK: Oh! Why?

CHAS: Everybody's talking about the Death Watch. They're rearing
their heads everywhere, it seems. And it's said that the
headquarters of the whole boiling shoot are right here. That's
what made the Valley hit the headlines.

DEREK: I suspected that all along. I got the settlers to form themselves
into a Vigilance Corps at today's meeting. They've made me
Commandant and appointed you as officer, by the way. No
objection, I suppose?

CHAS: I suppose not. A bit boy scoutish, but necessary, no doubt. So
long as I don't have to drill. Ugh! By the way, I ran into Peter
Spelter in Joh'burg.

DEREK: Peter flourishing?

CHAS: Seems to be. But I'm afraid there's a bust up coming.

DEREK: What do you mean?

CHAS: I've no evidence, but all the same I'm positive he's had a tip
about Trenterley and Daphne.

DEREK: Say anything?

51

CHAS: No, just a look when Trenterleys' name cropped up. But what a look.

DEREK: (Fills and light pipe) Peter could be a pretty tough customer.

CHAS: So I was trying to convince Daphne.

DEREK: Did she need to be convinced?

CHAS: She laughed at the very idea.

DEREK: She's a little fool, that woman.

CHAS: Oh, yes, she's a fool right enough, but all the same I sincerely hope that Peter doesn't come down on the war path. It would be just too bad for all three.

DEREK: I reserve my sympathies for Spelter.

CHAS: Oh! I don't know, Derek. People are what they are, and do what they must.

DEREK: Scarcely a workable philosophy, if I might say so.

CHAS: It's damned easy for a man to condemn others when he is free from the same temptation.

DEREK: That's meant for me, I take it. How the devil do you know what my temptations are?

CHAS: Well, if the thought isn't irreverent, I hope to God one sunny day you fall with a bang and a clatter. That would even things up a bit. (Rises) I must go and wash. (Exit R).

          (DEREK lights pipe. Enter VIVIEN)

DEREK: Hullo, darling. I've been wondering where you'd got to. You're not looking well.

VIV: I'm all right.

DEREK: A bit down in the dumps?

VIV: No, I wouldn't say that. (<u>Leans against chair</u>). Derek, do you remember Sybil Selwyn, my stage friend?

DEREK: Sybil? Sybil? Oh yes, I remember. A svelte creature who sidles up like a one-eyed rat.

VIV: Derek, how can you? That's a perfectly beastly thing to say and quite unjust.

DEREK: (<u>Smiling</u>) Very likely. After all, I can't be sure that I've ever even seen a one-eyed rat.

VIV: You're horrid.

DEREK: What about dear Sybil, anyway?

VIV: I've had a letter from her. She's at Capetown. Her company's on an African tour and she wants to know if she can come here for a few days before they begin.

DEREK: Oh, does she?

VIV: You don't mind, do you?

DEREK: Why should I?

VIV: You don't seem very keen.

DEREK: (<u>Rises, puts pipe on ashtray</u>) Not keen, perhaps, but perfectly willing. I thought her a rather mischief-making type, but of course you know her very much better than I do.

VIV: (<u>Rises – on verge of hysteria</u>) Mischief-making type! Oh, Derek dear! Sybil represents all that's gay and sane and poised and bracing in the great world outside. Don't you sense her strength and vitality?

DEREK: (Approaches her a step or two) Frankly, no. I must be allergic.

VIV: Why she's awfully attractive, especially to men.

DEREK: Doesn't make my mind dance with thoughts of spring.

VIV: Why, she's a most stimulating person; heaps of men have told me so.

DEREK: In that case you had better keep her away from Trenterley, or he may break a blood-vessel.

VIV: I believe you're against her because she's an actress.

DEREK: Rubbish, fond heart, sheet unadulterated rubbish. What's wrong with actresses? You surely remember that my mother was an actress. And a damned good one. What is more I nearly married an actress – who's right at the top of the tree today.

VIV: What happened? Did you find her too frivolous? Or did she deem you too worthy?

DEREK: Neither, she threw me over because I was too harum-scarum.

VIV: Don't make me laugh. Too harum-scarum indeed.

DEREK: The truth, Vi.

VIV: Is that how you would describe yourself now?

DEREK: Of course not, you donkey. One grows up – and takes root. We all have to do that in time, you know, even you.

VIV: (Rushes to him sobbing) Takes root! Oh, Derek darling, I can't, I can't.

DEREK: Darling, whatever has gone wrong? Sit down and get it off your chest, there's a dear. Come on, tell me.

           (Derek puts her on settee and sits with her)

VIV: (<u>Making an effort</u>) Derek, you must take me away from here at once. Do you hear, at once.

DEREK: Farming doesn't run to long holidays, my dear. We've only been back six months and in that time we've had ten days each in Durban and at the Cape, to say nothing of the trip to the Falls. If you want another change, I'll arrange it of course. But not for myself.

VIV: No, no, you must come too.

DEREK: I can't, old girl. The farm needs me here. And so does the settlement. Damn it all, darling, with a native rebellion brewing – Is that what's worrying you?

VIV: No, but – Oh, Derek, for God's sake come away. Sell the farm and let's go and live in some pleasant civilised place.

DEREK: No, darling, I can't. I'd do anything for you, but – (<u>Rises and moves away</u>).

VIV: Not that. I see. Even though I'm desperate. You love your trees and things more than you love me.

DEREK: No.

VIV: You must do. I know it's a big thing to ask, but if you put me first you'd do it for me.

DEREK: At this moment I love you more than anything else in creation. But if I gave way to you now I'd despise myself later on. And not only myself. Don't forget I've worked here for fourteen years.

VIV: Then it's quite hopeless. (<u>Jumps up in desperation</u>). Can't you see that this place is driving me mad? Oh, you're so unimaginative and hard. (<u>Up to stoep. Derek goes to her – hand on her shoulder</u>).

DEREK: Do <u>you</u> love <u>me?</u> Enough to listen carefully to me for just two minutes?

VIV: Of course, Derek. But nothing you say –
(<u>Derek takes her on to stoep</u>).

DEREK: Look! You see those orchards on that mound? (<u>She nods</u>). Well, I even made the mound. Fourteen years ago, all that was a swamp. I made those citrous plantations, and behind the house is the market garden and poultry farm. Fourteen years ago, all this land (<u>sweeps with his hand all round</u>) was wilderness – a sheer heartbreaking wilderness of prickly pear and mimosa. Look at it now, I created all this. Do you think it was easy? Do you think I don't know what solitude and monotony are? (<u>Bringing her to settee again and sits</u>). Come and sit down and I'll tell you. When I first came here, I was the only white man. During the months I was building this house and clearing the bush, I talked to no one except natives. I lived in a tent. And night after night for nearly a year, I sat by myself listening to hyaenas. And that wasn't all. The development company promised to have the irrigation dam ready in a year. It wasn't ready for two years. But I'd planted in preparation for the water at the end of the first year. It didn't come. What did come was the drought. It broke me. All the planting ruined. My small capital was exhausted. I went and got a job on the mines – underground. For nine months I didn't buy one thing I could do without. I didn't drink and I didn't smoke. I saved every penny. At the end of that time I had enough to buy a levelling machine. I brought it here. Other settlers had come to the Valley by then. I hired myself and my machine to them, so that in my spare time I could use the income to clear away the bush which had begun to grow again on my land. I had just got a second lot of crops and trees planted when the locusts came. Three times I started all over again. But now – there's the reward. I'm not boasting. I'm simply telling you so that you will understand my feelings when you ask me to give it all up. (<u>On to the settee</u>). Listen, Vivien. If you will only try and make something grow out there – no matter how small – if you will only plant it and look after it and even in a sense live for it – then you will get the rhythm of the soil inside you and you'll begin to know real

56

happiness. (<u>Vivien is looking up at him</u>) Will you try, darling? (<u>Rises then speaks</u>)

(<u>Vivien rises slowly – nods – then impulsively embraces him and he kisses her</u>).

<u>CURTAIN</u>

ACT TWO

SCENE TWO

**The same. One month later. Evening. Lights off.
(Vivien & Sybil standing at outer door. They turn and leisurely saunter towards sofa. Sybil has a slanting walk).**

SYBIL: One thing I can say about this previous Valley, it knows how to stage a sunset. Wish my lights man were here to pick up a few wrinkles. (Drops into seat). The evening seems to be the only tolerable part of the day in Africa.

VIV: Yes. And sometimes the very early morning. But the evenings are best, except there's so much melancholy in their beauty.

SYBIL: You're not happy here, Vivien, are you?

VIV: Is it as obvious as all that? Or are you psychic?

SYBIL: It's obvious enough.

VIV: (Sits down and takes out cigarette case) Cigarette?

SYBIL: To please you, my dear. Can't say the brand appeals to me.

VIV: (Lighting up) Oh, I don't know. African cigarettes grow on one (enter JIM) Jimmy thinks Boar tobacco heavenly, don't you Jimmy?

JIMMY: Takes a bit of getting used to. Like Africa. But it gets you in time. Africa does that, too.

SYBIL: Vivien won't applaud that remark, will you Vi? Though Vera Felton undoubtedly would.

VIV: I suppose Africa has an appeal for men which few women understand.

SYBIL: It hasn't much appeal for your brother-in-law. Or for Lord George Trenterley, if it comes to that. I think George is too delightful for words. He might have stepped straight out of an Edwardian comedy. I'm so glad he and Charles have decided to come with us on our tour. They'll brighten things up considerably. That reminds me, I had better be getting ready. One case is already packed. Would you be a dear, Jimmy and carry it out for me? Trent will be here any minute now.

JIMMY: With pleasure. Did you say that Charles is going with you?

VIV: Sybil persuaded him this afternoon.

JIMMY: H'm. Well, I'll lug your cases outside for you (Exit)

SYBIL: Nice boy, Jimmy.

VIV: Yes, a bit serious, but decidedly nice. It's rather a blow, your taking Charles. This place will be pretty dull without him. And in troublous days it's comforting to know that there are men around.

SYBIL: Are you quite sure you won't come with us? (Vivien shakes her head) Not even until all this Beetle business has blown over?

VIV: Blown over! My dear, its been going on for months, and its getting worse, not better. It's more like Mau Mau every day.

SYBIL: The worse it becomes, the sooner it will be over, surely. Who knows what the situation will be in a couple of months' time?

VIV: No Sybil, I must stay with Derek.

SYBIL: But Derek can't want to have you here at the present time.

VIV: He thinks in terms of the Voortrekkers' wives.

SYBIL: Voortrekkers?

VIV: Dutch Pioneers. Their wives re-loaded their guns in battles with the Zulus.

SYBIL: Antediluvien. (<u>car noise in distance</u>) Would that be George Trenterley's car? I must finish my packing.

VIV: I'll give you a hand. (<u>Exeunt. Enter Derek. Goes to desk, sits writing and smoking. Knock on outer door</u>).

DEREK: Come in. (<u>enter TRENTERLEY. Derek rises</u>). Oh, its you, Trenterley.

TRENT: Ah, I was hoping to catch you alone.

DEREK: Take a seat (<u>Trent sits</u>) You are off today, I gather?

TRENT: Yes, I'm taking a jaunt round the country with Miss Selwyn's company. In fact, I've called to collect her now, but I'd rather like a word with you first.

DEREK: What can I do for you? (<u>Sits</u>)

TRENT: Well, I have a proposition which will tempt you, I believe. I have never been under any delusion that you have an excessive regard for me, in fact, I have every reason to suppose that you would give a good deal for me to clear out of Leopard Valley. Am I right?

DEREK: What we think of each other doesn't matter two hoots. What is your proposition?

TRENT: Well, assuming that I'm right, here's your chance to get rid of me.

DEREK: What chance?

TRENT: I am offering to sell you my farm. (<u>Derek laughs</u>) I assure you I'm quite serious.

DEREK: Oh, I don't doubt that. What tickled me was your description of sixty acres of derelict land as a farm.

TRENT: Yes, perhaps that was an exaggeration, but even so it is good land and could make a first rate farm.

DEREK: I agree.

TRENT: Then how about it?

DEREK: Not on your life, Trenterley.

TRENT: I bought it for £100 an acre, £6,000 in all. I'll sell for £5,000.

DEREK: Sorry.

TRENT: For £4,500 then.

DEREK: No, Trenterley, I'm sorry. For one thing I have neither the money nor the time. For another thing –

TRENT: Yes?

DEREK: Forget it. In any case, I can't accept your offer, so that's all there is to it.

TRENT: That's a damned nuisance. I don't want the thing. It's a mill stone around my neck.

DEREK: It needn't be a mill stone.

TRENT: What do you advise?

DEREK: You really want to know?

TRENT: Of course, my dear chap. I'm at my wits end.

DEREK: Very well. Go back, take off your coat, and get down to the job of making your farm something different from a rather unpleasant joke. You could transform the whole place in five years. I understand that you have some private means to keep you going.

TRENT: Awfully nice of you to put it so delicately. My gracious sire pays me the miserable sum of £800 a year on the condition that I live in Africa.

DEREK: Cheer up. He'll soon be driven by high taxation to come out here himself, and then he'll pay you £800 a year to live in England. However, in the meantime you've got a chance to make you farm yield a profit.

TRENT: Thank you very much.

DEREK: Why the devil did you take the land if you hadn't the guts to farm it?

TRENT: Private reasons, old boy. However, I can see I'm wasting your time. I appreciate your advice, even though I don't propose to act on it. No, my dear Romley, farming is all very well for people like you, who have the pioneering spirit, and a romantic feeling for the soil. Through many generations my family has become less and less capable of attending to practical affairs, until now it is purely ornamental.

DEREK: So that's how you regard yourself, is it – as an ornament?

TRENT: Precisely, old boy. An ornament. A flower of civilisation. Of course I suppose that like the rest of mankind I sprang originally from the soil, but my aversion to it makes me think it happened many billions of aeons ago. After all, the rose springs from the soil, but I don't suppose it is exactly proud of its origin.

DEREK: Well, I'll leave you to answer for the rose. Now, if you'll excuse me? (<u>Rises</u>)

TRENT: Duties on the farm, eh? You know, Romley, I cannot for the life of me understand your passion – I might almost call it lust – to be eternally fussing over the soil. I suspect some deep psychological reason. Doubtless Freud has a word for it.

DEREK: It would be highly diverting to be psycho-analysed by you, Trenterley, but I'm afraid water-leading has first claim and it's nearly time.

TRENT: (Rises) Well, I'm sorry you have not availed yourself of the opportunity of getting shot of me. As it is, there will be nothing for it but for me to show my smiling face again in the Valley.

DEREK: In that case, I wonder if you will let me say something that I have been wanting to say to you for some time.

TRENT: (Sits on edge of table) This is where I groan. Fire ahead.

DEREK: It's simply this. If you do come back, I should strongly advise you to start a different mode of life.

TRENT: I shall, my dear fellow. I shall become founder and first president of the Leopard Valley Sunday School Guild.

DEREK: My warning is serious, Trenterley.

TRENT: (Approaches Derek) If we are to talk seriously, Romley, I must tell you to keep your nose out of my affairs. You are not charged with the custody of my soul, you know.

DEREK: I'm afraid I don't care twopence about your soul, and I don't really know why I should worry twopence about your life.

TRENT: My life?

DEREK: I believe your life to be in danger.

TRENT: (Laughs) You have a nice taste in melodrama. I suppose you think Peter Spelter intends to pounce upon me. (Chuckles and moves away) Mild little Peter.

DEREK: Spelter is not so mild, if it comes to that. But I was not thinking of him. These are troublesome times in the Valley, Trenterley. If I were you, I would watch things from the native angle. There have been rumours from Songeti's reserve about you.

TRENT: And you listen to filthy rumours?

DEREK: Trenterley, there is some reason to suppose those "filthy" rumours are true. And if they are true, they accurately describe a very filthy state of affairs. I suppose you know the maximum penalty prescribed by the law for tampering with native women?

TRENT: (Somewhat threateningly) This is preposterous.

DEREK: Preposterous is the word.

(Trenterley is about to give vent to his feelings when JIMMY enters – remains on stoep)

DEREK: Yes, Jimmy?

(Trent moves away – scowling)

JIMMY: Oh, hullo, I didn't know you were engaged. I just came to ask you if you would give Brutus the once-over before I saddle him.

DEREK: Of course. Excuse me, Trenterley, and don't forget what I have said.

TRENT: On the contrary, it shall lie next to my heart with all the precepts offered to me in the nursery. (Exit Derek with lantern – then Jimmy)

(Trent gives an exclamation, crosses to …..)
(Enter VIVIEN from R)

VIV: Hullo, Trent, have you come to say good-bye?

TRENT: Not to you, my dear. Sybil said she was going to persuade you to come with us.

VIV: She's very anxious for me to, but I don't think I can. Do sit down.

            (They sit. Trenterley sits next to Viv)

TRENT: You'll be foolish to stay. I say that as a friend.

VIV: Oh? Why?

TRENT: Well, my dear, what you want is a break. You're looking jaded, not half the woman you were when you first came to the Valley. Besides…

VIV: Yes?

TRENT: I was going to say something about your husband. Do you mind?

VIV: Well?

TRENT: Derek is the most estimable fellow, but I expect you find him a little overpowering.

VIV: Why should I?

TRENT: Why should you? Great Scott, the fellow takes an interest even in my soul! He must keep yours in a positive hot-house. He was getting at me just before you came in.

VIV: Whatever about?

TRENT: Oh, just about my way of life. Lecturing me for my own good, I suppose he would call it.

VIV: How jolly! And do you feel the benefit?

TRENT: (<u>Makes a gesture</u>) You know, he not only can't see my point of view, he can't bring himself to believe that I have a point of view.

VIV: I'm not sure I know what your point of view is, myself, Trent. Won't you tell me?

TRENT: Heavens alive! What a question to answer when a man is stone cold sober. I'll tell you what. Charles is coming, isn't he? (<u>She nods</u>). Good! He can drive my car. We'll put Sybil in the front with him. We'll sit at the back, and as we speed through the moonlit night I'll explain my philosophy of life to you.

VIV: (<u>Laughing</u>) How do I know that you may not decide to put me in front while you let Sybil into the secrets of your philosophy?

TRENT: My dear girl!

VIV: You can scarcely deny that you have a roaming disposition, you know.

TRENT: That's just what I would explain.

VIV: Since I'm not coming, I'm afraid you'll have to explain it now… or not at all.

TRENT: Well, how shall I put it? You see, every man has to do the best he can in life. Some choose toil and – er – perspiration. Like Derek, for instance. Derek suppresses his desires by taking it out of the soil. A grand fellow, Derek, but a slave. Now others, like myself, have more courage.

VIV: More courage?

TRENT: That is what I said. Oh, I don't mean the kid of courage which fights with fear. I mean the unconscious courage which simply short-circuits fear – soars above it. Only people with this kind of courage are free.

VIV: Free to wander from one affair to another?

TRENT: That is stating it rather crudely, Vi.

VIV: But accurately?

TRENT: Free also to remain put, if that is what one happens to want. Everything is a choice between pain and pleasure, and as I see it, only a madman chooses pain.

VIV: I should have thought that a Don Juan reputation would have been rather a stumbling block to a life of pleasure. Doesn't it make woman look at you askance?

TRENT: Not a bit of it. Women find it most alluring.

VIV: That surprises me.

TRENT: Does it, Vivian? Truthfully? Can you honestly say you find nothing alluring in my reputation? (<u>Trent rises and goes to her. Viv is silent</u>). Come on! You have made me confess. What about a spot of confession from you? Do you or don't you find my reputation alluring?

VIV: (<u>Pause</u>) No. In any case, I don't understand why women should allow themselves to be deceived. I suppose you always make a vow of eternal devotion to each one of them in turn.

TRENT: Of course!

VIV: And they fall for it?

TRENT: Yes, the vanity of women is incredible.

VIV: Thank God, I should never be such a fool.

TRENT: Then you would be a fool indeed.

VIV: Whatever do you mean?

TRENT: I mean, that should I make a vow to you, it would be the plain unvarnished truth. Ever since I first set eyes on you I have adored you.

VIV: What do I do now, Trent? You have had more experience than I. Swoon into your arms?

TRENT: I mean what I say, Vivien, and I'll prove it to you. We'll go on this tour with Sybil, but we won't return. Let's go to Europe. Italy, first, Vivien. Italy or Leopard Valley? Civilised people, or black rebels? Peace and colour and beauty or the drabness of farm life stretching away into the infinite future? That's the choice, Vivien. (Viv puts hands to her cheeks, rises and moves up. Trent to her) Listen, damn it... I love you, I swear it. Derek will let you have a divorce, and then we'll marry and settle down somewhere on the Mediterranean coast. You'll never, never adjust yourself to this third rate Colonial existence. Face up to it. I'll look after you for the rest of your life – on my solemn word of honour. (He tries to kiss her – she slips on to the stoep, looking off).

VIV: Good God, here's Derek coming (Down to Trent) Listen, Trent, I don't want Derek to find us together. I know – (Hurries to door R) Come and help with Sybil's luggage, quick, this way.

(Exit Vivien and Trenterley R)

(DEREK enters – stands on stoep looking round, then comes down to desk as CHARLES enters from up R and speaks from stoep)

CHAS: Derek – can I speak to you a minute? It's something important.

DEREK: Of course. (Chas hangs hat up. Derek comes down R.C.) But don't forget, I've got to lead water at seven. What's wrong?

CHAS: I'm through, Derek. I can't stand it any longer. I must get away at once (Comes down) (Pause) I'm sorry, old man, you won't understand, but there it is.

68

DEREK: Sit down. (Chas sits, leaning forward). You're wrong, Charles. I do understand.

CHAS: And you're not mad with me?

DEREK: No, Charles, I'm not mad with you. I'm disappointed, of course, and terribly sorry. I had hoped you'd have liked the life. Its damn bad luck on you that you don't.

CHAS: God, it's decent of you to put it like that. I'm afraid I have misjudged you.

DEREK: (Sits on edge of table) I've felt sorry for you all along. But it was useless to let you see it so long as you had any hope of settling down. It was your own battle, and I couldn't help. Of course, I've been sorry for you. But I'm also damned anxious about you, old man. You're mistaken if you blame your environments altogether, you know. You loathed your trips to town, don't forget. The unrest is in you, and it's quite as likely to take hold of you in London as in Leopard Valley.

CHAS: Yes, I know that. God, yes. But all the same, it's got me by the throat, and it tells me to clear out tonight or else – blow my brains out. (Pause)

DEREK: What are you going to do?

CHAS: So far as my immediate plans are concerned, I'm going off with Sybil Selwyn tonight. A man's gone ill in her company, and she thinks she can wangle me into the job. That'll be a start.

DEREK: You're not emotionally entangled, are you?

CHAS: Not in the least.

DEREK: I'm glad, she wouldn't be any use to you, and I gather Trenterley's interested there.

CHAS: Yes, he's coming too. Going to accompany the tour and see Africa. Say's he'll try and get his company floated while he's away.

DEREK: I hope he goes for good. Don't have much to do with the fellow, Charles. Nasty bit of work.

CHAS: I know, but he's good company. (Pause) It's only fair to warn you that he's trying to persuade Vivien to come along as well. (Pause) I'd speak to her if I were you.

DEREK: I shall do nothing of the kind. If I can't trust my own wife it's a poor look out, don't you think?

CHAS: Well, I've told you. (Pause)

(Derek moves up and returns)

DEREK: What about your four thousand? Will you leave that invested in the farm? I'll guarantee the interest, of course.

CHAS: I was coming to that. Derek – I'm sorry, but I want it.

DEREK: I suppose it's no good telling you it's safer where it is?

CHAS: I know it is. But I want it, all the same.

DEREK: We've got just over two thousand five hundred in the bank. I was going to buy another tractor with it, and perhaps invest in that bull the Settlement is too damned silly to buy. (Crosses slowly to R.O.) Well its goodbye to all that. For some years at all events.

CHAS: I'm sorry, Derek.

DEREK: So am I, because I've an instinct your little inheritance is going west as soon as you get hold of it.

CHAS: So have I. I'm sorry, Derek, but there it is.

DEREK: I'll arrange for an overdraft tomorrow, unless I post-date a cheque to the end of the quarter.

CHAS: That will do nicely, Derek. I've got enough ready cash.

DEREK: (Going to desk and takes out cheque book) Very well. (Sits and writes cheque. CHAS rises and moves up).

CHAS: I can't tell you how damned decent you've been.

DEREK: (Rising and hands him cheque) Don't try. Here it is.

CHAS: Thank you, Derek.

DEREK: Now I must get busy water-leading. (Picks up hat from desk) Goodbye.

(They shake hands)

CHAS: Goodbye. I'm really very, very sorry.

DEREK: I understand. (Exits)

(Chas moves down R.C. as Sybil and Trenterley enter from L)

CHAS: Hullo, Sybil.

SYBIL: Delivered your ultimatum?

CHAS: I've said goodbye, if that is what you mean.

SYBIL: You'll feel like a new man, Charles. Besides, you ought to make a damn good actor.

TRENT: What about me?

SYBIL: So long as there's an eternal triangle, there'll always be the part of the other angle for you to play. I hope we manage to persuade Vivien to come too. I've half convinced her. She's pining away here. She wasn't intended to carry the White

Man's Burden any more than you two were. If she gets a break now she'll be able to sort herself out and decide what she really thinks about the mud and head and Beetles of this ghastly hole.

CHAS: I told Derek that you were both trying to persuade her.

TRENT: My dear fellow, what on earth did you do that for?

CHAS: Common decency, I suppose.

SYBIL: I told him myself, as a matter of fact.

CHAS: Really! What did he say?

SYBIL: Declined to intervene. Left it entirely to her. I asked him if he had any objection. He said he objected most strongly, but wouldn't do anything about it. If she decided to go she could and would.

TRENT: He's coming on, is our good Derek. May blossom out himself one day. Become the gay Lothario of Leopard Valley, what?

CHAS: Shut up, Trenterley.

TRENT: Hullo, hullo, that family loyalty of yours again?

CHAS: I know this. Your pants – or mine, for that matter, are not good enough for Derek's boots to kick (<u>Enter Vivien from R</u>) Hullo, Vi. I've fixed up with Derek. It wasn't so bad as I thought. He was jolly decent about it. I could have wept. (<u>Leans against table</u>).

VIV: I know that side of Derek. It's what keeps me here.

SYBIL: But you are coming away for the trip, aren't you? Vi, darling? You know it will do you all the good in the world.

TRENT: Of course you're coming, Vi.

VIV: No.

72

TRENT: What nonsense.

VIV: (Sits centre) I'm not coming.

SYBIL: You'll go completely barmy if you stay here, what with Beetles and things.

VIV: I know. It's too horrible for words. But I've got a duty to Derek after all.

SYBIL: It's not party of a wife's duty to worry herself into an asylum. I'll help you to get ready, Vi. Derek says he'll place no obstacle in the way of your holiday so why worry. (A knock. Enter VERA. SYBIL up to her) Oh, hullo, Vera. Charles has fixed it up. He's coming tonight with us. We're trying to persuade Vi.

VERA: Congratulations, Charles.

CHAS: You congratulate me?

VERA: I do. I've heard that Songeti's men have been gun running. They've got hundreds of rifles hidden in the bush. There's going to be Hell on earth here soon. You'll just about get away in time.

TRENT: Dash it all, you aren't seriously suggesting that anybody's running away from a log of niggers.

CHAS: Well, it helps to lend me speed. I'm not enamoured of the prospect of an assegai in the back every time I go outside.

VERA: You're supremely honest, Charles. I'll say that for you. But otherwise I haven't an ounce of respect for you – running out on your brother after the job he's made of taming this wilderness.

CHAS: (Jumping up) But I don't want to tame the damned wilderness Felton darling. Why uproot a decent God-fearing wilderness to make room for English snobberies and English adulteries.

VERA: Don't speak to me like that. I'm not a snob and I'm not an adulterer.

CHAS: Heaven forbid! (<u>Moves down R</u>)

VERA: And although there is some snobbery in the Settlement, I doubt whether there's any adultery here.

CHAS: Oho!

VERA: How can there be, when there's a Board official testing all the milk that goes out? However, that's beside the point. The Valley will probably be well rid of you both – you especially, Trenterley.

TRENT: Charmed, I'm sure.

VERA: But you're not going to let Derek down, Vi? You're going to stay?

SYBIL: Vi will make her own choice.

VERA: Where's Derek? Water-leading?

CHAS: Yes.

VERA: Then I'll go and have a word with him. I'll tell him to keep his prize cockerels locked up, in case there's anything else our Miss Sybil wishes to abduct. I'm sure you must have a perfectly smashing part for a prize cockerel, haven't you?

SYBIL: I expect we could write one in.

VERA: Why stop at cockerels? What has Cabbage done to be left out? Quite sure you don't want Cabbage as well, Sybil? You seem to be expending your company into a global corporation. Why not go the whole hog. What's wrong with Jimmy de Lisle? What's wrong with Derek Romley? Come to think of it, what's wrong with me? Why not let me play Moth or Mustard Seed. What

74

part will you give Trenterley? Puck, perhaps? Or Oberon, or even Madam Butterfly?

TRENT: Here, I say!

SYBIL: We must draw the line somewhere, Vera dear. Sorry to disappoint you, but acting would hardly be in your line. One needs a certain amount of subtlety on the stage.

VERA: Subtlety! Is that what you'd call Trenterley – subtle? Is that how you see yourself? A person of fine discrimination? In that case the elephants in the Mambo Bush are creatures of the most exquisite sensibility. I must let Derek in on the subtlety joke. But first let me tell you this, Sybil – I think what you are proposing to Vivien is damnable, absolutely damnable. (Exits)

SYBIL: Charming creature, isn't she?

CHAS: (Approaches Viv, she rises) We'd better go before Derek comes. We don't want a row.

TRENT: We do not. Ready, Vi?

VIV: I'm staying here.

SYBIL: Vi! I've got some of your own things packed and in the car.

VIV: I know if I went with you I should probably never come back.

TRENT: Nonsense, my dear girl.

CHAS: I understand that exactly, Vi. Look! You know our first address. Join us if you change your mind, as you will.

VIV: Very well. (Chas shakes hands. Gets hat and waits on stoep. Sybil kisses her and joins Chas).

TRENT: I'll give you a hand with your kit, Charles. (Crosses to Viv and takes her hand) We'll expect you soon, Vi. Cheerio, my dear.

(Exit Sybil, Chas and Trent chatting and laughing. Viv looks round and shudders, then moves up to….. Pauses then turns and stands petrified as CABBAGE enters L wearing blanket. Gives a sinister smile. Viv presses back against jamb)

VIV: Get out.

CAB: (Sinister) Oh, yes. (Grins and exits).

VIV: God! I can't, I can't! (Rushes out)

(Enter DEREK and VERA)

DEREK: Where's Vi? (Calls Vi) (Rushes out R and returns) She's gone! (Sound of car driving off)

<u>CURTAIN</u>

ACT TWO

SCENE THREE

A week later, NIGHT. Lights on. Sound of steps on the gravel, then of a halt and swing-round, and then the steps are heard again.

JIMMY enters from L putting revolver in holster. DEREK sits on settee, looking through papers and smoking.

DEREK: What's up Jim?

JIM: Need you ask? Songeti spy in the lucerne field again. By Jove, I'll be glad when the tension's over.

DEREK: Have a drink?

JIM: I certainly will. (<u>Gets drink</u>) Chapman says that Songeti's location has doubled in size the last few days. Every jail bird and skellum in the Rand is finding refuge there. I wish the Balloon would go up and bust. Cheers (<u>Derek responds</u>) (<u>drinks</u>) Why the hell don't the police go in and get the man. (<u>Sits R.C.</u>)

DEREK: Songeti's been clever. Even white juries require evidence, to say nothing of white judges.

JIM: They've got some evidence.

DEREK: Only for smaller indictments. They want to get him for good and all when they do move.

JIM: Must they wait for new murders to be committed in the hope of getting the bigger evidence? What about gun running and

77

illegal possession of arms? He could get ten years for that, and ten years is a breather.

DEREK: (Rises and puts papers on desk and comes down R.C.) You wouldn't find a gun in the place. They are too well hidden in the bush.

JIM: But surely the police have spies in the location?

DEREK: They're spotted the moment they get in. Songeti's intelligence service is amazing.

JIM: Well, I don't know, it beats me. What's he got in his mind? He must know that native rebellions can't succeed against European armaments. Tanks and aeroplanes and things.

DEREK: He's obviously a fanatic.

JIM: But fanatics are realists as a rule. He must have some objective in his head.

DEREK: (Crosses to C and paces about) Yes, I agree. And I'd like to find out. In fact, I'd give a lot for a few minutes conversation with our friend Songeti. But he's as elusive as hell and refuses to see even the authorities. Ah, well, there's nothing to do but hang on, I suppose, and keep our own people up to the mark. Thank God we've got the women and children in the larger farmsteads.

JIM: What about Vera Felton? Did you get her off peacefully to the Drift Hotel this afternoon?

DEREK: I almost had to carry her.

JIM: What an Amazon she is.

DEREK: (Crosses thoughtfully to R) She's a grand person.

JIM: She'll never stay at the Drift. I bet she'll go back to her own place tonight.

DEREK: I don't think so. She knows that you and I are taking turns to keep guard at the Drift all night and that if she comes home we'll have to divide up and get no sleep at all.

(Crunching on gravel off L. Jimmy to stoep. Derek rises and puts R.H. in pocket)

JIM: Nevertheless, she won't stay at the Drift. Hullo! (shouts, moving hand to holster) Hullo!

(VERA enters with rucksack)

VERA: Hullo, blokes.

DEREK: What the blazes are you doing out at this time of night? You're mad.

VERA: You're telling me. The night is full of creepy, crawly beetles.

DEREK: Then why did you come, you incorrigible fathead.

VERA: Sheer softness of head and kindness of heart. You two are not getting enough food and nowhere near enough sleep. You can't go on like this. I've come to look after you.

DEREK: You don't mean you've come to stay here?

VERA: I do. Brought pyjamas and all. No use arguing. The rest of my kit will follow tomorrow.

DEREK: But what about that reputation of yours?

VERA: My good man, they can't say I'm a coward. The Drift Hotel is safe, as you'll agree.

DEREK: But it isn't a question of cowardice.

VERA: You mean the general fuss people make about men and women's sleeping arrangements. That's always struck me as absurd. Why, before I came to Africa I went on a trip all over the continent with my own brother, and I didn't care a damn what anybody said or thought. (<u>Jimmy and Derek exchange looks and Jimmy moves to rails to look out</u>) Which room, Derek?

DEREK: You win. Charles's old room.

VERA: Good, I'll turn in, I'm tired. But I'm getting up at two and taking your watch at the Drift. I'm not going to have you worn out.

DEREK: You will do nothing of the kind.

VERA: Why not? You've taught me to use a gun, and I don't suppose I'd be any more scared than a man would be.

DEREK: Out of the question, but I appreciate your guts.

VERA: Then make use of me, you silly ass.

DEREK: It's a man's job at the Drift.

VERA: I'm not going to stay here all night arguing. I'll show you, though. (<u>Jimmy to....</u>) I'm going to the Drift at two whatever you may say, and if you've any sense you'll say in bed and sleep. Be good. (<u>Exit L</u>)

BOTH: Cheerio, Vera.

JIM: (<u>Comes down L.C. Derek sits</u>) What a woman!

DEREK: Unbeatable!

JIM: Marvellous settler's wife she'd make. If only... (<u>Pauses. Derek puffs at his pipe</u>)

DEREK: If only what?

JIM: If only she wasn't so completely sexless. (<u>Derek says nothing</u>) I don't suppose she's ever given sex one thought in her whole

80

life. (<u>Derek still says nothing</u>) Well, it's nearly ten. I'll get down to the Drift. See you at two. So long.

(<u>JIMMY puts hat on and exits R of stoep</u>)

DEREK: I'll be there.

(<u>DEREK sits smoking – then stiffens and SONGETI enters.</u>
<u>Watches door L wearing blanket</u>)

DEREK: What can I do for you, my friend?

SONGETI: That is encouraging. Had you been true to type, you would have said "Get out of my home, you bloody nigger."

DEREK: That would have been foolish of me. I've wanted to have a talk with you for a long time. If I am not mistaken, you are Chief Songeti?

SONGETI: I am that chief. And I have long desired to meet you. Are you not the leader and the backbone of the white man in these parts? I come out of respect for you to tell you with my own lips that you must die.

DEREK: Very charming of you.

SONGETI: I did not expect you to be disconcerted.

DEREK: You speak remarkably good English. You must have gone to a damn fine Mission School.

SONGETI: My Alma Mater would be flattered.

DEREK: No flattery, I assure you, it's true.

SONGETI: I don't mean that. I mean that Oxford would be flattered to hear itself described as a Mission School.

81

DEREK: Oxford? Then what in Hell's name are you doing organising the whole criminal riff-raff of Africa. Is that all that Oxford offered you?

SONGETI: No, I would not say that. But it showed me where my quarrel lay with your people.

DEREK: What quarrel, precisely?

SONGETI: One small indication of it is that here, in my own country, I must stand in your presence – the presence of an intruder.

DEREK: Are you suggesting that you should sit down? I didn't know a man was expected to entertain his own executioner.

SONGETI: I shall stand.

DEREK: You said this was your own country, by the way. Is it? Is it any more yours than mine? The white people came here over the sea at the same time that yours arrived out of the north. And the Bushman and the Hottentots who were here first got a better deal from us, I think.

SONGETI: You are wrong. We gave them the better treatment.

DEREK: What! Why, you butchered them wholesale.

SONGETI: Death was preferable to what you have given them – and us. In death there is dignity.

DEREK: Oh, I know about all the slums and squalor and vice in the great cities.

SONGETI: That is not my quarrel. A strong people can survive poverty and shake off vice, because vice is an open enemy. Let me tell you my quarrel. It is that you have allowed a great squalor of the spirit to submerge your own country and flood into Africa, submerging the beauty and the laughter and the pattern of the African soul. The white people have become the Lords of Cheapness, the Sovereign Kings of the vulgarity which soils

82

and corrupts and destroys the beauty of the world. Against that I do raise the standards of the Black Revolt. Against that do I summon the people of Africa to gnaw into your rottenness as the Death Watch Beetle gnaws into rotten wood.

DEREK: And the Lords of nobility are the rascals you have gathered in your camp?

SONGETI: They are what the Whites have made them. Even they can be ennobled in battle.

DEREK: Poor devils! What chance have they against guns and aeroplanes?

SONGETI: I will tell you. We shall lose now, and that defeat shall be a victory, because it will be a beacon for the future. We must have martyrs; we must forever keep alive the warrior spirit of our people, for when that dies, bastardisation is complete. That is the final degradation.

DEREK: Well, you're certainly going to have martyrs in plenty, including yourself.

SONGETI: Yes, when the fire burns upon that mountain (points off) the day of martyrdom will dawn. If I can make my escape, I shall, for my work will not be finished. If not – (shrugs).

DEREK: It is all madness, Songeti. Criminal madness.

SONGETI: You see no more in it than that?

DEREK: (Puts hand in pocket. Pausing). Yes, I see more in it than that, but criminal madness it still remains.

SONGETI: I hoped you would understand a little. I hope you will now understand why you must die. Your death will electrify my followers through the Valley.

DEREK: Flattered, I'm sure.

SONGETI: I have too much respect for you to seek to flatter you. Will you die on your feet?

DEREK: Well, inside this pocket, I have a finger on the trigger of my gun, you know. And you don't appear to be armed. You are not going to kill me by magic, are you?

SONGETI: You are a brave man, and I salute you. (Salaams) I say again, will you die on your feet?

DEREK: (Rises and whips out revolver) Songeti, I'm beginning to think you ought to be in an asylum. You are coming with me to the police post. (SONGETI backs up on the stoep and DEREK follows. CABBAGE creeps in L door – wearing blanket. He raises assegai and is about to throw – SHOT from L. CABBAGE falls and SONGETI slips out. VERA enters in dressing gown carrying revolver).
Good God! Cabbage! Jove. So that was it, Songeti. Well, Vera.

VERA: I thought I heard somebody creeping through the house. Lucky you taught me to use this.

DEREK: M'yes! You've saved my life right enough.

VERA: That's not much to write home about, is it?

CURTAIN

ACT THREE

SCENE ONE

Same as Act 1. Several weeks later. Morning.
DEREK enters wearing topee and hurries to phone.

DEREK: (<u>'phoning</u>) Conservancy Board, please. Again? Damn! (<u>Replaces receiver, puts topee on desk and wipes forehead. Enter JIMMY from.... Wearing hat</u>) They've cut the wires.

JIM: What wires? (Removes hat and holds it under arm)

DEREK: The Conservancy Board. I must find out why van Rooyen's not sending down water supplies. Everything is baked.

JIM: I came in to tell you. Chapman's just returned from the mountains. He found the Conservancy Offices looted and not a sign of van Rooyen.

DEREK: Good God! Another?

JIM: It looks like it.

DEREK: (<u>Down R.C.</u>) This is the last straw. If the Government delay any longer I shall go to Pretoria and raise Hell.

JIM: The police are pouring into the Valley from all over the Union, complete with machine guns too. They've decided to move.

DEREK: They must do more than arrive and hang about. They must walk in at once. (<u>Up to opposite Jimmy</u>) Get down to the Company office, old man, and tell them to call a meeting of Settlers for this afternoon. Rebellion or no rebellion, we've got to get the water down or it'll mean ruin for dozens of people.

JIM:	I'll go at once. (<u>Puts on hat and exits. Derek sits at desk and writes. VIVIEN enters from L</u>)
DEREK:	Vivien!
VIV:	Yes, Derek, I've come back.
DEREK:	As abruptly as you went away.
VIV:	I explained in my letter that sudden departure, I wrote to you from Bulawayo, you remember.
DEREK:	Yes.
VIV:	You made no comment on it.
DEREK:	No comment seemed necessary – or even possible.
VIV:	(<u>Breaking down</u>) Oh Derek, I was an awful coward.
DEREK:	(<u>Going to her</u>) Nerves are tricky things my dear. Come, sit down. (<u>Leads her to settee</u>) There, that's better. (<u>Sits on chair</u>) Have you come back alone?
VIV:	No, Charles and George Trenterley are here too.
DEREK:	They've left you to break the ice, I take it.
VIV:	Charles is talking to Vera at the gate. George has driven to his own place to dump his kit, but he's coming along in a few minutes. I asked him to dinner.
DEREK:	Did he accept?
VIV:	Of course, why shouldn't he?
DEREK:	How very jolly!
VIV:	I don't understand, Derek. Oh! Oh, surely you don't think –

DEREK: No, of course not. It's simply that Trenterley knows damned well that he's not popular in this house.

VIV: Oh, come Derek. It's silly to have feuds. The Bulawayo papers say that open rebellion may be expected any day now. You should be glad to have Trenterley back to lend a hand.

DEREK: My word yes. He'll be worth a couple of Guards Divisions.

VIV: I don't really see any need to be sarcastic.

DEREK: No? Very well, my dear, let's talk of something else. What topic do you suggest?

VIV: Why are you so distant, Derek? Come and sit here. (<u>Derek, after a pause, moves to settee</u>).

DEREK: Well?

VIV: Are you glad to see me?

DEREK: (<u>Pausing</u>) In one way, (<u>pausing again</u>) But not altogether. No, to be perfectly honest I am not altogether glad (<u>Vi lowers her head</u>) I'm sorry my dear, but I must be truthful with you.

VIV: Then you – you don't love me any more?

DEREK: That is a very difficult question. I don't know how to answer it. How to distinguish between love and desire. I do desire you, Vi.

VIV: But you do not respect me?

DEREK: I do not respect you, Vi, unless you are able to say you do not love me.

VIV: Why should you respect me if I say that?

DEREK: Because love which allows a woman to run away from a man as
            you ran away from me, when I was in need of you, doesn't
            strike me as being particularly worthy of respect.

VIV: But Derek, I was terrified.

DEREK: No doubt. I'm not blaming you.

VIV: Darling, I don't understand.

DEREK: Then damn it all, Vivien, it's time you tried to understand.
            (Turns away in exasperation)

VIV: But you've just said you don't blame me.

DEREK: I don't blame you, my dear, but neither do I excuse you. I
            simply see you for what you are.

VIV: And what am I?

DEREK: A woman of very little courage.

VIV: You say that after I've come back to you?

DEREK: The emotional whirl which brought you back is quite likely to
            take you off again.

VIV: (Jumps up) You're a beast. I can't think how I ever came to fall
            in love with you.

DEREK: I am now inclined to think that you fell in love with an
            opportunity to escape from a not very congenial home.

VIV: Oh!

DEREK: Why not be honest with yourself, Vivien?

VIV: Tell myself that I have no courage or staying power! Make
            myself out to be an opportunist!

DEREK: At least admit to yourself that you failed appallingly as a wife, and that you are entirely selfish and self-absorbed. Do you remember my suggesting you should try and make something grow?

VIV: So that's it! I've let you down, because I refused to become one of your damned farm-labourers.

DEREK: Forgive me, Vivien. I was a fool to suppose that a conversation like this would ever get us anywhere (Vi weeps. Derek approaches. She pushes him off and rushes out R door)
(Enter Charles from L)
(Derek who had been watching Vivien rush out, turns wearily to greet him)
Oh, the prodigal brother.

CHAS: None other. (Derek rises and shakes hands) We've decided to come back and give the Valley another trial)
(Hangs up hat)

DEREK: The Valley's in luck.

CHAS: Good of you to say so.

DEREK: I didn't quite gather from Vivien why you've come.

CHAS: Vi and I decided that we'd be curs if we threw our hands in without having another shot. The Valley didn't seem quite so bad when we were away from it.

DEREK: Yes. From the Valley's point of view even Trenterley seemed tolerable when he was completely out of sight.

CHAS: Derek – everything was absolutely straight. She lost no time in letting Trenterley know where he got off.

DEREK: That's enough. (Moves down R.C.)

CHAS: I'm sorry. (Follows slowly) By the way, it's only fair to tell you that I've fallen for Vi myself.

DEREK: I thought you might.

CHAS: It was partly why we came back.

DEREK: I see. Makes things a bit complicated, doesn't it?

CHAS: Oh, I didn't suggest coming back here.

DEREK: What are you going to do?

CHAS: Trenterley's putting me in as his manager.

DEREK: I see. I hope you get paid.

CHAS: He's formed his company.

DEREK: Indeed, who's he soaked? Not you, I suppose (Chase is silent) Has he? Have you parted with your four thousand?

CHAS: (Shamefaced) Most of it. When I was tight. When I'm tight, I become beautifully trusting. I see the world through a haze of good fellowship, I'm afraid.

DEREK: Charles, you unbelievable idiot. How could you do it, however drunk?

CHAS: He offered me the manager's job.

DEREK: Does one expect to pay a bribe of four thousand pounds for a job?

CHAS: It isn't a bribe.

DEREK: Besides, did he tell you that the farm's mortgaged for over five thousand?

CHAS: Good God! Are you sure?

DEREK: No doubt about it. Quick, tell me – when did you part with your cheque?

CHAS: Yesterday.

DEREK: Is it cashed?

CHAS: Can't be. You may remember you post-dated it to the end of the quarter.

DEREK: So I did. Good. Did you make it payable to him or to this bogus company?

CHAS: To him.

DEREK: Good. (Turns and listens – then hurries to stoep and looks off L) Here he is. (Chas moves up) Go and keep Vi away from this room until I've done with Trenterley. Send him in at once and don't say why.

CHAS: But –

DEREK: Hurry, you fool, do you think I'm going to argue? Get out and do what you're told.

CHAS: Right. (Snatches hat and rushes out. Derek paces up and down. TRENTERLEY enters and holds out hand).

TRENT: Hullo, Romley. Delighted to see you again.

DEREK: (Ignoring hand) Your delight is one-sided.

TRENT: If that's your mood, perhaps you would like me to go.

DEREK: Nothing better. (Trent turns to go) But not for a moment. (He turns around) Hand me that cheque you have in your pocket.

TRENT: My dear fellow! What title have you to any cheque of mine?

DEREK: I want that cheque Charles gave you, and I'm going to get it.

TRENT: I think not. That cheque is my legal property. Or at any rate, the Company's of which I'm Chairman. It's been paid over in return for shares.

DEREK: You stand on legality?

TRENT: I do.

DEREK: With a bogus company?

TRENT: The company is not bogus.

DEREK: Properly formed, eh?

TRENT: Properly formed, to acquire farm property which, you will scarcely deny, exists.

DEREK: Excellent. Does there also exist a mortgage on that property to the tune of five thousand pounds?

TRENT: Certainly not.

DEREK: So that Chapman and quite a few others are guilty of forging bonds, eh? (Trent is silent) You liar!

TRENT: It's not criminal to mortgage ones property.

DEREK: But criminal not to disclose the fact in selling it. And there's not a word about it in your prospectus. Hand over the cheque.

TRENT: I'm damned if I will.

DEREK: That's a pity, because I can't force you.

           (DEREK goes to phone)

TRENT: What are you going to do?

DEREK: You've never done a stroke of work in your life, about time you began.

TRENT: You mean –

DEREK: Precisely – the Police. (<u>Trent takes out wallet and hands cheque</u>
            <u>to Derek</u>) That's one account settled. Now get out. (<u>Points to</u>
            <u>door L. Trent shrugs and exits L as Vera enters</u>).

FIRE ON MOUNTAIN

VERA: Hullo, Derek, I've seen Charles and he told me the news.

DEREK: Yes, Vera. Vi is back. (<u>There is silence</u>)

VERA: I do hope it will be all right this time, Derek. I'm sorry to give
            you a shock. But unless the rain comes there will be ruin in the
            Valley.

DEREK: Oh, it's not as bad as that. We'll get the water down from the
            dam somehow.

VERA: Derek, a gang of Songeti's Death Watch men have smuggled in
            some dynamite and blown the dam to Hell!

DEREK: The dam blown up? (<u>Gives gesture of despair and moves up to</u>
            <u>stoep. VERA puts foot on step</u>)

VERA: The waters took the western slopes and flooded the Canger
            Valley. And there's something else, did Songeti say something
            about a fire on the mountain? Look over there.

DEREK: Yes, that means the rebellion's begun at last.

            (<u>VERA hits her leg nervously – crosses to … as JIMMY rushes</u>
            <u>in from ….</u>)

JIM: By Jove, Derek, see that fire! The balloon's gone up all right.
            I've just come down from Chapman's. The Beetles haven't a
            chance. Police! Why, I've never seen so many in my life.
            Armed to the teeth. They're absolutely all over the place.
            Songeti's location must be completely encircled and shut off,
            except on the bush side.

DEREK: Oh, that's already covered. During the night, Zulu and Shangaan police detachments have been penetrating the bush. No escape that way.

JIM: Chapman says the hut-tax is the issue.

DEREK: Yes, I heard it was to be. Songeti said he'd defy the authorities to come and collect it.

JIM: And so half the police in the country are going in response to the invitation. Thank Heaven it's come to a head. Much bloodshed, do you suppose?

DEREK: Likely to be appalling. Songeti has told his men that the police bullets will turn to water, and they believe him. (<u>Comes down C Jimmy follows</u>)

VERA: Tell me, Derek – I've had this on my mind to ask you for a long time – just how much are we to blame for things like this?

DEREK: You mean that in the widest sense, I suppose?

JIM: Ha! You've been reading some of the English newspapers.

VERA: Yes, I have. A lot of people at home do seem to be picking on the Whiteman in Africa, you'll agree.

JIM: Too true.

VERA: What's the answer, Derek?

DEREK: There's no simple answer, Vera.

VERA: Have we any right to be in Africa?

DEREK: As much right as we have to be in England.

VERA: You mean that our ancestors came to England.

DEREK: Quite so. Almost everybody in the world is where he is because he or his forebears went there from somewhere else.

JIM: Migration to America, Canada, Australia and so on?

DEREK: Not only that. Migrations to Russia, Japan, France, India. From the beginning of recorded time people have moved here and there about the earth. Where would we three be, would we even be born, if our fathers had stayed locked up in their little island, if they had refused the challenge of the seas?

VERA: That's not all there is to it, though, Derek.

DEREK: What else?

VERA: When things go bad, as they are tending to do now in Africa, is the blame not ours?

DEREK: "Blame" is rather a facile word. "Responsibility" perhaps.

JIM: Why the distinction?

DEREK: Because when two or more races meet and try to settle down side by side, the pattern of their relationship is not willed. It is something that happens. That stands to reason, don't you think? Even our relationships with our own friends and neighbours are not willed – not, at any rate, for the most part. I don't will myself to detest Trenterley. Or to like – who shall we say? – Peter Spelter.

VERA: Yes, I see what you mean. But responsibility for our attitude towards them remains our own?

DEREK: Precisely. And God knows there's wide enough scope for wisdom and tolerance.

VERA: Ah, tolerance!

DEREK: Why do you say "Ah, tolerance"? One does not tolerate a spear aimed at one's throat, Vera. Or the dynamiting of a dam which keeps both White and Black in the Valley alive. (<u>To Jim</u>) Heard about the dam?

JIM: Yes, Chapman told me. Pretty serious, I gather.

DEREK: If we don't get rain very soon, it means ruin.

JIM: Whew! What a life! Still, you can't say it isn't exciting. Oh, that reminds me, there's another thing.

DEREK: Yes?

JIM: Oh, Vera, I wonder if you'd let me tell this to Derek by himself?

VERA: Of course, I'll see to lunch (<u>Exit L door</u>)

DEREK: Well?

JIM: I thought I ought to tell you. On my way back from Chapman's I saw a man come out of Trenterley's house – a white man. What struck me as jolly queer was, he carried something in his hand. He chucked it into the lucerne field before he came to the road. I didn't see what it was, but the image of a gun formed itself in my mind.

DEREK: Know the man?

JIM: Never seen him before. A decent sort of chap, I should think. I said "Good Morning" as we passed. He returned the greeting with a cheerful grin. But –

DEREK: But what?

JIM: Well, I remember something Charles once told me about Daphne's husband. This fellow had a look of absolute steel in his eyes.

DEREK: Small, sandy fellow?

JIM: That's right, with a short military moustache.

DEREK: Peter Spelter, all right.

JIM: Suppose it was a revolver!

DEREK: My God! (Paces up and down) Look, Jim. You were quite right not to say anything in front of Vera. Vera's perfectly okay, of course, but we must keep this entirely to ourselves. Agreed?

JIM: Why, of course.

DEREK: Pretend to be surprised if the news should come.

JIM: I get the idea.

DEREK: Where's Charles, by the way?

JIM: I passed him as I came along. I expect he was going to Trenterley's.

DEREK: Did he see Spelter?

JIM: No, Spelter went in the other direction, towards Chapman's.

DEREK: Good (Enter CHARLES) Oh, here he is.

CHAS: Give me a drink for God's sake!

(Crosses and sits. Mops his face. Derek gets him a drink. Jimmy to   ).

DEREK: Of course. (Gives him drink) You look shaken.

CHAS: The sight I've seen would shake anyone. Trenterley's dead.

DEREK: What!

JIM: Dead!

CHAS: The Death Watch got him. (<u>Derek looks at Jimmy and nods</u>) I went along not suspecting a thing. God, what a sight! Spear wounds, by the look of them.

Ghastly! His body was in the hall.

DEREK: Spear wounds!

CHAS: That's what they looked like.

DEREK: Queer. Do you know the difference between spear wounds and wounds made by a gun?

CHAS: No, I don't suppose I do, at a glance. Spear wounds came to mind, that's all.

DEREK: Anybody about?

CHAS: Not a soul. There's a grisly sort of silence over the whole Valley. Poor old Trenterley. Needn't worry about his prospectus now. Nor about Peter Spelter. The Beetles have done Peter's work for him right enough.

DEREK: The Beetles have got something coming <u>to them</u> very soon. Come, Jim, lets go and keep an eye on things. I don't think they can possibly break through the police cordons, but just in case... (<u>gets hat and makes sure he has revolver</u>) Help yourself to another drink, Charles.

CHAS: Thanks, I will.

DEREK: And I shouldn't say anything to Vi for the time being, if I were you.

CHAS: Right, I won't (<u>Exit Derek and Jimmy. Chas rises and refills glass. VIVIEN enters from R door carrying hat</u>).

VIV: All alone?

CHAS: Hullo, Vi, darling. Isn't all this too ghastly for words?

98

VIV: What, particularly?

CHAS: Well – er, oh, the general tension. The hush in the Valley is enough to drive one mad; everywhere silent little groups of armed police, to say nothing of the Mounted Rifles – all waiting. I've heard the Durban Light Infantry are working up the Valley from the South. Things should happen any moment now. Ugh! Horrible! (Drains glass)

VIV: But when things have happened, there'll be peace again in the Valley. That'll be something.

          (Vivien sits with a sign. Puts hat on table)

CHAS: Peace in the Valley – oh, God. Peace in the Valley! An endless desert of days! Peace in the Valley – the small talk, the drought, the irritability, the – the death in life. It's no good, Vi, darling.

VIV: I know. I knew this morning, when I talked to Derek. He was – impossible.

CHAS: So far as you and I are concerned, yes, he does seem impossible. What did he say?

VIV: Oh, he was so strong and set and clear-cut and Olympian. He'd never appreciate what it cost us – to come back as we did.

CHAS: I think he would. I half hinted (VIVEN gives a startled exclamation) No, only my own feelings. Not a word about yours. He seemed to think it quite natural. I believe he's summed up the position all right.

VIV: Then perhaps that's why he spoke to me as he did. But in that case he might have given us credit for the gesture we made in returning.

CHAS: He would, if we kept it up. Don't let us fool ourselves, my dear. We're not really generous people who can throw more than a sop to our consciences. We can plan a great gesture; but that's all. We can't keep it up. Our feelings master us. We're the products of our age – as neurotic and unstable as Hell. We may get better one day. I believe we shall. But at present we're not cut out for endurance. Let's face it. Let's take the plunge, today.

VIV: After only an hour?

CHAS: Yes, after only an hour. It will be easier now than later. Easier for everybody.

VIV: Easier for Derek?

CHAS: Yes, above all easier for Derek. He'll be relieved, Vi. Whatever he goes through, he'll still be relieved. At the back of his mind he knows that you will never grow into the kind of wife he had hoped. And he won't put you to the degradation of being – what shall I say? – Used?

VIV: He has injured my pride enough already.

CHAS: No, my darling. Do please let us be honest. That injury is self-inflicted. We may be unstable, we may be cowardly, but at least we won't try to pretend we're the injured parties. We'll catch the mid-day train and this time we'll never come back – unless one day we can come and visit him without a consciousness of being the wash-outs that we are.

VIV: You've almost macabre truthfulness about you, Charles. Should I be able to live up to it? If Derek reproaches me with spiritual cowardice, won't you be reproaching me with intellectual cowardice?

CHAS: Don't be silly, darling. Let's go now, before the bullets begin to fly.

VIV: (Rises) You are quite sure that Derek will be glad?

CHAS: Fundamentally, yes. I am sure of that. It will be the removal of an impediment.

VIV: Impediment to what?

CHAS: To a tolerable contentment.

VIV: Charles, dear, you don't think he's in love with anybody else, do you? I've sometimes wondered about Vera Felton.

CHAS: The Virgin?

VIV: They're terrible fond of each other.

CHAS: I know. But Vera hasn't got an ounce of sex in her. You've noticed her farcical innocence. Sex is completely her blind spot. A psychologist would probably discover that she received some shock in girlhood, which made her mind automatically fashion a bastion against further shock. No, no I don't suppose Derek will remarry, and Vera certainly won't marry. Now then, young woman, will you or will you not elope with me?

VIV: Yes, Charles. I won't dither this time.

CHAS: Do you love me?

VIV: Derek said this morning that he found it difficult to distinguish between love and desire. It is difficult, I think. All I know is that I want to get right away from Africa and that I want to go with you. That will have to do for the present.

CHAS: It is enough. (Approaches to C) Kiss me.

VIV: Not in Derek's house, Charles.

          (Charles ignores the protest and kisses her)

CHAS: The better the house, the better the deed. (Kisses her again. DEREK appears on the stoep. Stands looking at them without visible emotion. Vivien turns and sees him and breaks away).

VIV: Oh, God! (Pause) We are going, Derek. Please don't say anything.

CHAS: Nonsense. You had better say what you've got to say, Derek.

101

DEREK: Sit down. (They hesitate). Sit down. (They sit) Any moment now, within a few hundred yards of this house, some scores of men are going to meet a violent death. I envy you your detachment.

CHAS: What the devil has that to do with the situation anyway?

DEREK: Very little, it seems. But all of us belong to the world; we all have at least some responsibility for what happens in it.

VIV: For God's sake come off your pedestal, Derek, even though you may be the only man on earth who can afford to live in a glass house.

CHAS: Yes, I must say Vi's right there, Derek. If only you had an ounce of human weakness in your make-up.

DEREK: Don't talk like a fool.

CHAS: I mean it. Life is very easy for a man like you, but not so easy for others you expect to measure by your own standards.

DEREK: You were at school at the time. Did you ever hear how I came to leave the Navy?

CHAS: Father said you relinquished your commission.

DEREK: I was court-martialled – dismissed the Service.

CHAS: What!

VIV: Derek!

DEREK: I was dismissed – when the war ended, I was in command of a M.G.B. By that time, I had acquired a taste for alcohol. I became a dipsomaniac. I got tight night after night, and after a bit day after day. I ended up in a blaze of triumph by throwing the code books overboard. That meant a court-martial. Mine is a somewhat vulnerable glass-house, I'm afraid, Vivien.

VIV: Oh, darling, if only I'd known (Rises and goes to him).

DEREK: What difference would that have made? One cannot regulate ones life by emotional flourishes, my dear. Don't try.

VIV: I'm afraid I should never understand you, Derek.

CHAS: (Leans forward and speaks quietly) Why did you tell us?

DEREK: Two reasons. First, to answer the pedestal taunt. Second, to show that people like you and I, Charles – (Chas sits up without looking at him) people with a tendency to go off the rails – require to make some pretty strict rules for ourselves, if we are not to come to a sticky end.

VIV: It's a bit late in the day to spare me, Derek. Why not include me among the people inclined to go off the rails.

DEREK: Because to go off the rails, implies being on some rails to start with, and having some individual momentum of ones own.

VIV: That's insulting.

DEREK: I'm sorry if you think so. However, lets come to the business in hand, which is, I suppose, that you two are proposing to elope.

CHAS: Not after what you've just said.

DEREK: My dear Charles, please don't behave like a sentimental ass. Nothing I have told you can alter the fundamental situation. Before you go off, Vivien, let me apologise for my part in the fiasco. I should have had more sense than to hurry you into marrying me, and then bring you to a place like this. I shouldn't have assumed that you'd like it here. I'm sorry, Vi.

VIV: (Almost weeping) Derek! That was sweet of you.

DEREK: You know, I think you two will have a chance together. You're more suited to each other. My trouble is that I see points of view too damn clearly. I see, for instance, that if I have the right to put my own way of life above my wife's she has the right to do the same thing. And it's bad to be able to see a thing like that so clearly. Lovers should not have too much logic in them. I make a dashed bad lover, I'm afraid. Good luck to you both. (Shakes hands with Vivien. She picks up hat and goes to stoep as Charles shakes hands and moves to go)

(As Charles is about to go out, Derek calls him back)

DEREK: Charles! You didn't come back to collect this. (Holds out cheque)

CHAS: You got it back? Thank Heaven!

DEREK: I should tear it up if I were you.

CHAS: Thanks awfully, Derek. He would have cashed it yesterday, but for you. Well, goodbye, and thanks for being so decent. Come on Vi. (Exits and holds door off).

DEREK: Goodbye, Vi, and good luck. (Viv hesitates, then hurries off followed by Charles).

(Enter VERA L door)

DEREK: They've gone, Vera. Thought they would.

VERA: Vi?

DEREK: Yes, with Charles – and with my blessing.

VERA: Your blessing! Well, all this love and marriage business is a closed book to me. I simply don't understand it. The point is – are you terrible cut up, as you were last time?

DEREK: No, I cannot honestly say that I am.

VERA: That's a mercy, anyway.

(Enter Jimmy on to stoep)

JIM: It's just on eleven. I wish they hadn't ordered the settlers to stay
            at home and guard their own farms. I'd love to be in it,
            wouldn't you?

DEREK: I would not.

JIM: You wouldn't? Why? I'd give anything to be in the fun.

DEREK: I've outlived all that, I'm afraid. Poor devils! Police bullets will
            turn to water, indeed. Will they Hell!

JIM: But hang it all, it isn't as though the Death Watch were
            innocent.

DEREK: What is innocence? Or guilt? Or scoundralism? Or idealism?
            I've given it all up long ago and content myself with making
            orange trees grow. And the drought won't be allowing me to do
            that much longer.

            (DISTANT SHOTS)

JIM: Hullo! (Jimmy turns to rails – shading his eyes – and Vera joins
            him. Derek goes and sits, head in hands. VERA turns and looks
            at him)

CURTAIN

ACT THREE

SCENE TWO

Same evening. Lights On. Wireless set down L. DEREK at rails – looking up. VERA is leaning against jamb. Crop and hat on table.

DEREK: Do you know, I think it looks as if salvation is at hand.

VERA: Rain?

DEREK: Yes, rain. Cross your fingers and hope like hell.

VERA: Hoping waters no crops. How many times have the clouds come, only to pass over.

DEREK: Everything's parched. Baked. If the rain doesn't come tonight, we're done. Start at the beginning again, eh? Well, not quite – but nearly.

VERA: Still game?

DEREK: Yes, but there's no virtue in being game. It's our living, there's nothing else to do. However, come away, in case watched clouds never burst.

VERA: (Comes down L.C. Derek follows – C)
           What's the latest about the rebellion?

DEREK: Nothing now. It's smashed into smithereens, as it had to be.

VERA: Casualties?

DEREK: Only seven of our men, six police and one mounted infantryman. But on the other side! Two hundred and fourteen of the poor benighted fools wiped off the face of the earth.

106

Seven hundred wounded and Heaven knows how many prisoners. The whole lot, I suppose.

VERA: Except Songeti.

DEREK: Except Songeti. He's still at large. But not for long. He can't get far, wherever he's hiding. There are police on every farm, watching out for him. In fact, there's a Zulu policeman in our kitchen at the moment, cooking our dinner. He kindly volunteered. And there are more in the barn. Songeti hasn't a hope in Hell.

VERA: It must be a horrible feeling to be hunted.

DEREK: I suppose so. But I've got no sympathy to waste. I'm afraid. At least, not much.

VERA: Some?

DEREK: Yes, some. Can you tell the difference between a crazed fanatic and a saint?

VERA: Well, I suppose saints don't go out on the kill.

DEREK: Don't you believe it. Saints have bathed the earth in blood for no more than the whiff of an idea. I find myself less and less capable of delivering judgment about these things, at any rate of apportioning the blame. There's no line to be drawn, as far as I can see. (<u>Moves up to stoep</u>) Well, well – is that the rain never coming?

VERA: (<u>Moves up to front of steps</u>) Take your silly mind off the rain. (<u>Pause</u>) I slipped over to see Daphne this afternoon.

DEREK: Did you?

VERA: What do you think? Peter's at home.

DEREK: Is he? Anything said about Trenterley?

VERA: They hadn't heard a thing 'till I told them.

DEREK: H'm!

VERA: In fact, Peter seemed frankly incredulous. I had to repeat it three times before he'd believe that Trenterley was really dead. Then he appeared absolutely flabbergasted.

DEREK: Curious!

VERA: What's curious?

DEREK: (Comes down) Oh – life. What do you think of our wireless set? As soon as Vivien got back, I phoned and ordered one for her. They delivered it this afternoon.

VERA: Tried it yet? (Crosses to wireless)

DEREK: Not yet. (RAIN) Vera, listen! (Pause, then both run on to stoep) Thank God! The rain.

VERA: The rain! (Both dance and laugh shouting 'Rain'. Derek suddenly clasps Vera and kisses her)

DEREK: (Still holding her) The rain. (Kisses her again).

VERA: I say –

DEREK: What a Godsend! I'll go and make sure the tanks are open. (Rushes out)

           (Vera comes down and switches on wireless. Gradually MUSIC fades in as she sits. Relaxes. Shoots her legs out and looks at them. Rises, crosses to mirror and studies herself, then hurries out R)

           (SONGETI creeps in from left. Peers in at window and enters. Stands looking curiously at wireless. DEREK appears and points to Police "to stay")

DEREK: What on earth? Songeti!

SONGETI: I am that man.

DEREK: Why have you come here? (<u>Switches off wireless</u>)

SONGETI: To hold speech with you, Whiteman.

DEREK: What there was to say, Songeti, has already been said – by the guns.

SONGETI: There yet remains a word to say.

DEREK: No word that can bring the dead to life.

SONGETI: I thought, Whiteman, that you understood a little. We spoke together that night, you remember. Has it all gone from your mind, that understanding?

DEREK: You have killed many men, Songeti.

SONGETI: And do Whitemen kill nobody? Two great wars in my own life – were they not wars of the Whiteman?

DEREK: Yes, they were wars of the Whiteman. But they were not fought in Leopard Valley, Songeti. And the men who made them were not answerable to the laws of this land, as you and I are answerable.

SONGETI: But you understood my purpose, for that is what you said.

DEREK: Yes, I understood your purpose and I told you it was madness.

SONGETI: You had respect for my vision.

DEREK: That is as may be. I grant no more than this – that although you have done much evil, I see you not as an evil man, but as a man insane.

SONGETI: I knew what I was doing.

DEREK: Oh yes, indeed. You knew what you were doing. You are not legally insane. But you are insane. Now tell me, why have you come to me?

SONGETI: I repeat, you are the only Whiteman in Africa who understands me. I come to seek your clemency.

DEREK: My clemency! That settles it. You are mad. This time we shall take that journey together to the police station.

SONGETI: I am hunted like a rat and there is no escape open to me, except one.

DEREK: There is no escape now, Songeti. (<u>Covers him with revolver</u>)

SONGETI: I repeat, there is still one escape. I cannot get out of this Valley by myself. My one hope is for you to drive me out in your car.

DEREK: (<u>Laughs</u>) God! After armed rebellion against my people, after attempting my own life, you expect me to take you for a joy ride round Africa! Come Songeti, I can't waste time.

SONGETI: I say I came to seek your clemency.

DEREK: I have none. You will come now.

SONGETI: I have come to offer terms.

DEREK: Terms, indeed. (<u>Approaches a few steps</u>)

SONGETI: Very well. I shall have many charges to answer, I know, charges upon they will hang me, but there is one charge I shall repudiate.

DEREK: Leave that to your lawyers, I'm not interested.

SONGETI: Yes, white man, you are interested. The charge of murdering Lord George Trenterley. (<u>Derek stops</u>) I thought that might stop you. A spy saw that murder committed. And the same spy overheard the conversation in this house.

DEREK: I am not concerned with this matter, Songeti. Come.

SONGETI: But Mr Spelter is very much concerned with this matter.

(A long pause)

DEREK: Blackmail.

SONGETI: It is not the right word for affairs of state.

DEREK: Affairs of state! You have conducted no affairs of state. Affairs of the morgue, let us say.

SONGETI: As you like, Whiteman. But Mr Spelter is not in the morgue. Mr Peter Spelter is alive.

DEREK: I see. Supposing I do as you require – I know you will hold your tongue, but what guarantee have I that your spy will do the same?

SONGETI: A police bullet through the spy's heart this morning is your guarantee.

DEREK: You swear?

SONGETI: I swear. He's dead.

DEREK: Excellent. Come, Songeti.

SONGETI: (Backs away. Derek follows) You will take me?

DEREK: I will take you, but not far.

SONGETI: Far enough to escape?

DEREK: Far enough to escape from all your troubles.

SONGETI: I thank you.

DEREK: Songeti, I will not deceive you. You gave me a warning that evening, and now I will treat you with the same respect. Go through that door, and you will answer for your actions in a Court of Law.

SONGETI: And make your friend Spelter answer for his?

DEREK: No, Songeti. That will not happen. You tried to blackmail me with that threat, but whatever you threatened would make no difference. The police are outside at this moment, waiting for you.

SONGETI: So you are not frightened for your friend?

DEREK: No, I am not frightened for him. You make your threat for a good reason; you won't carry out that threat, because there is no good reason. You are too great for that, Songeti. Your crazy rebellion is smashed, and you won't swear away the life of a good man for mere revenge. You intend you own death to be too dignified. Am I right?

SONGETI: You are right. Then I will tell you this, white man. Your friend, Mr Spelter, did not kill Lord Trenterley.

DEREK: What?

SONGETI: No. He beat him very badly with his fists, but he did not kill him. The killing was done by my men. We had our own quarrel with Lord George Trenterley.

DEREK: (To himself) Oh, so Charles was right after all. (To Songeti) Thank you for telling me, and now…

SONGETI: I understand. (Moves up on to stoep and raises his hand high above his head in the Zulu salute). Inkoos!

           (Exits with great dignity. Sharp order heard. 'HALT' DEREK stands looking out. Enter VERA in evening dress. Looking very feminine and very sweet. Crosses to wireless and switches on. QUIET MUSIC. Then crosses to…)

VERA: Who was that man, Derek?

DEREK: Songeti.

VERA: So Songeti is caught.

DEREK: Yes, Songeti is caught.

VERA: You are upset.

DEREK: Songeti was not like those power crazed fiends of Mau Mau. He had something about him, something of quality, something of nobility, if you will. (Makes a gesture). However, he's off my hands. (Turns and comes down steps. Stops dead and stares at her) VERA!

VERA: Well? (Pause)

(DEREK hesitates – then approaches – flounders)

DEREK: Vera, why, I've never seen you like this, never.

VERA: No, Derek, you haven't. Did you think you never would?

DEREK: I had hoped. Tell me, Vera, tell me. All that innocence business?

VERA: Innocence business?

DEREK: Was it one huge leg pull?

VERA: (Brightly) Oh dear no, a girl must have her defences – especially in a place like this.

DEREK: Then it was a leg pull. One long, gorgeous act.

VERA: Nonsense, my dear boy, I told you Sybil Selwyn said I couldn't act – not enough subtlety. And although my defence held, it wasn't really very subtle, was it? (Derek begins to laugh. Vera joins in. They roar with laughter, until a lightning flash and clap

113

of thunder brings them to alert. Pause) Mind you, Derek, I don't want to spoil a good joke, but that defence reflects something inside me.

DEREK: (Gently) Would you not rather use the past tense?

VERA: (Slowly) Reflected? Yes, reflected. It reflected something inside me. But I want you to understand what it was all about.

DEREK: I think I do. In our personal lives, just as here in Leopard Valley, we labour through long years overcoming difficulties and trying to make our lives fruitful, but often there is a long drought, and everything within us becomes parched, like the wilderness beyond those mountains. (Going closer to her) And then, when hope is nearly dead – can you finish the metaphor?

VERA: Of course I can. And then, when hope is nearly dead there comes the rain. (Derek takes her hand and leads her up steps to look at the rain. The rain lashes down).

DEREK: This is no ordinary rain.

VERA: (Triumphantly) My darling, it's a cloudburst.

(They look at each other – and kiss)

CURTAIN

Appendix 1

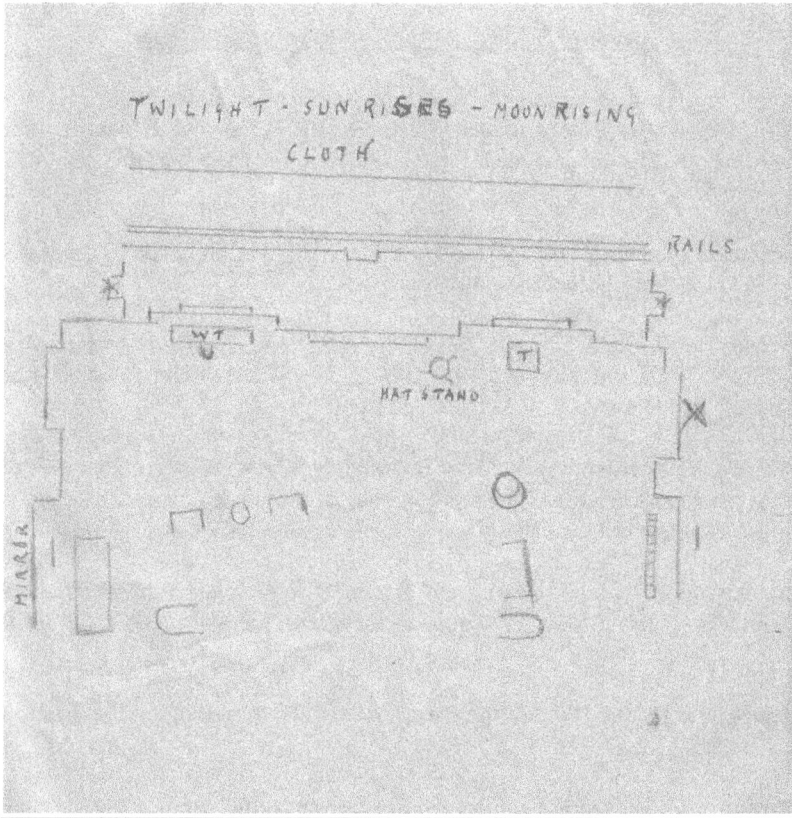

A.K. Chesterton's drawing of the stage setting.

Appendix 2

KING GEORGE V PRAISED HIS WORK

"Leopard Valley" Author's Adventurous Career

Two officers were booking seats at the Little Theatre when one of them noticed on the bill of next week's play, "Leopard Valley" by A.K. Chesterton.

"Ignorant blighters in this place," he remarked to his companion "They don't even know that Chesterton's initials are G.K.!"

When I told "A.K." about this little episode, he smiled – somewhat ruefully."What would you!" he exclaimed. "G.K. cast such a gigantic shadow that I can never hope to escape from it."

Mr A.K. Chesterton, who holds an important editorial position on the staff of the "Southport Guardian" has written two books on the theatre, as well as much dramatic criticism and some splendid tributes have come his way.

Reviewing one of his books, for instance, the journal of the Institute of Journalists acclaimed it as "equal to the finest literature." R.C. Sherriff wrote "A fine writer."

And James Bridle: "One of the most brilliant bits of writing on the theatre I have read."

Professor G. Wilson Knight, the Shakespearian critic, wrote: "His flashing images and periods of strong style make his work unique and much better than most good writing to-day."

Crowning tribute, though, was that of His late Majesty King George V. Archives of the Memorial Theatre at Stratford contain a letter from Sir Godfrey Thomas recording that the Duke of Windsor, then Prince of Wales, had read a piece of Chesterton's work to the King, who described it as "excellent."

When he became Editor of the "Shakespeare Review" some years ago, Mr Bernard Shaw disapproved of his "taking up the hobby of men who are born old." "There is something horrible in the thought that I once dandled a young fossil on my knee," wrote G.B.S.

"A.K." has had an adventurous career. In the last war he joined the Army as a boy of 16, fought in German East Africa and later on the Western Front. In 1922 he took up arms on the side of General Smuts' Government forces during the Witwatersrand Revolt. He dug for diamonds and worked on a gold mine before entering journalism.

He began writing plays in 1939, but the war came, and he forgot all about them for he was soon back in the Army. Although over 40, he volunteered for tropical service and a few months later was in the van of the British advance into Somaliland and Abyssinia. After reaching Addis Abbaba he was sent hurtling down to the coast to join the Somaliland Camel Corps for intervention in an inter-tribal war among the Somalis. It was in this affray that his health gave way, resulting in his being invalided out of the Service last year.

He attained captain's rank, and holds the Military Cross.

When I asked him how he felt to have one's first play about to be produced, he replied "In the ordinary way I imagine it would be torture, but I am lucky to have it staged by one of the finest producers in the country. I'm convinced that Mr Prentice and the Sheffield Rep (whose work I admire tremendously by the way) will do it as well as it can be done."

Southport Guardian, 18th March 1944.

Appendix 3

Produced last night at the Little Theatre for the first time on any stage, Mr A.K. Chesterton's play "Leopard Valley" had an encouragingly successful debut.

It engaged the interest immediately, and held it firmly to the final moment – a result very largely due to (as the author readily acknowledged) to the excellent performance by the Sheffield Repertory Company, whose task was not easy as there are one or two anticlimaxes.

The scene is the living room of a bungalow in the Leopard Valley Settlement, South Africa, and with its view of barren hills beyond fruit groves created by unremitting toil, forms an admirable setting for a theme which is not unfamiliar.

The characters, too, have been met with before – the settler who loves the soil, who wins fertility from the wilderness by undaunted effort, and who finds deep satisfaction in the job; his bride, fresh from England, adoring the place at the start but eventually nerve-wrecked by the dull monotony; his younger brother, restless and feckless; a titled wastrel, who pays more attention to his neighbours' wives than his farm; the fluffy grass-widow of a mining engineer; the enthusiastic young new settler; and the girl settler who has the same affinity with the land – and the same "guts" – as the pioneer.

You can pretty well guess how the story develops. It runs true to type, but its drama is sharpened and tensed by the menaces and crazy rebellion of a native confederation whose slogan is Africa for the Africans.

Cyril Luckham plays Derek Romley, the plucky pioneer, with convincing strength of purpose and character, but Enid Staff, as his discontented unstable wife, hardly brings sufficient emotional reaction to the role. Rachel Gurney is delightful as the naive, innocent girl-settler, and Myrtle Rowe's effervescing loquacity makes the bridge-party scene a gem. David Garth, Robert Wallace, Colin Dudley, Bruce Carstairs (a dignified rebel chief), Pamela Tiffen and Vint Graves all handle their parts excellently. Once again producer Herbert M. Prentice has done a first-rate job.

The Southport Visitor, 21st March 1944.

About A.K. Chesterton

Arthur Kenneth Chesterton was born at a South African gold mine where his father was an official in 1899.

In 1915 unhappy at school in England A.K. returned to South Africa. There and without the knowledge of his parents, and having exaggerated his age by four years he enlisted in the 5th South African Light Infantry.

Before his 17th birthday he had been in the thick of three battles in German East Africa. Later in the war he transferred as a commissioned officer to the Royal Fusiliers and served for the rest of the war on the Western Front being awarded the Military Cross in 1918 for conspicuous gallantry.

Between the wars A.K. first prospected for diamonds before becoming a journalist first in South Africa and then England. Alarmed at the economic chaos threatening Britain, he joined Sir Oswald Mosley in the B.U.F and became prominent in the movement. In 1938, he quarrelled with Mosley's policies and left the movement.

When the Second World War started he rejoined the army, volunteered for tropical service and went through all the hardships of the great push up from Kenya across the wilds of Jubaland through the desert of the Ogaden and into the remotest parts of Somalia. He was afterwards sent down the coast to join the Somaliland Camel Corps and intervene in the inter-tribal warfare among the Somalis.

In 1943 his health broke down and he was invalided out of the army with malaria and colitis, returning to journalism. In 1944, he became deputy editor and chief leader writer of *Truth*.

In the early 1950s A.K. established *Candour* and founded the League of Empire Loyalists which for some years made many colourful headlines in the press worldwide. He later took that organisation into The National Front, and served as its Chairman for a time.

A.K. Chesterton died in 1973.

About The A.K. Chesterton Trust

The A.K. Chesterton Trust was formed by Colin Todd and the late Miss. Rosine de Bounevialle in January 1996 to succeed and continue the work of the now defunct Candour Publishing Co.

The objects of the Trust are stated as follows:

"To promote and expound the principles of A.K. Chesterton which are defined as being to demonstrate the power of, and to combat the power of International Finance, and to promote the National Sovereignty of the British World."

Our aims include:

- *Maintaining and expanding the range of material relevant to A.K. Chesterton and his associates throughout his life.*
- *To preserve and keep in print important works on British Nationalism in order to educate the current generation of our people.*
- *The maintenance and recovery of the sovereign independence of the British Peoples throughout the world.*
- *The strengthening of the spiritual and material bonds between the British Peoples throughout the world.*
- *The resurgence at home and abroad of the British spirit.*

We will raise funds by way of merchandising and donations.

We ask that our friends make provision for *The A.K. Chesterton Trust* in their wills.

The A.K. Chesterton Trust has a **duty** to keep *Candour* in the ring and punching.

CANDOUR: To defend national sovereignty against the menace of international finance.

CANDOUR: To serve as a link between Britons all over the world in protest against the surrender of their world heritage.

Subscribe to Candour

CANDOUR SUBSCRIPTION RATES FOR 10 ISSUES.

U.K. £25.00
Europe 40 Euros.
Rest of the World £35.00.
USA $50.00.

All Airmail. Cheque's and Postal Orders, £'s Sterling only, made payable to *The A.K. Chesterton Trust.* (Others, please send cash by **secure post**, $ bills or Euro notes.)

Payment by Paypal is available. Please see our website at **www.candour.org.uk** for more information.

Candour Back Issues

Back issues are available. 1960 to the present.

Please request our back issue catalogue by sending your name and address with two 1st class stamps to:

The A.K. Chesterton Trust, BM Candour, London, WC1N 3XX, UK

Alternatively, see our website at **www.candour.org.uk** where you can order a growing selection on-line.

www.ingramcontent.com/pod-product-compliance
Lightning Source LLC
Chambersburg PA
CBHW030419100426
42812CB00028B/3020/J